GUIDE
TO GREECE

21 March 2019

GUIDE TO GREECE

POEMS

GEORGE KALOGERIS

George Kalogeris

LOUISIANA STATE UNIVERSITY PRESS

BATON ROUGE

Published by Louisiana State University Press
Manufactured in the United States of America

Designer: Laura Roubique Gleason
Typeface: Minion Pro
Printer and binder: LSI

Library of Congress Cataloging-in-Publication Data
Names: Kalogeris, George, author.
Title: Guide to Greece : poems / George Kalogeris.
Description: Baton Rouge : Louisiana State University Press, [2018] |
    Includes bibliographical references.
Identifiers: LCCN 2017056656 | ISBN 978-0-8071-6841-7 (pbk. : alk. paper) |
    ISBN 978-0-8071-6842-4 (pdf) | ISBN 978-0-8071-6843-1 (epub)
Classification: LCC PR6061.A56 A6 2018 | DDC 821/.914—dc23
LC record available at https://lccn.loc.gov/2017056656

in memory of my parents

For Ted,

With enormous
admiration for
your magnificent
poems — a genuine
Master.

Love,

George

But one way or another the world will go on being the place of epiphanies. And, to travel among them, literature will be the last surviving Pausanias.

—Roberto Calasso, *Literature and the Gods*

Even Pausanias was puzzled.

—Roberto Calasso, *Tiepolo Pink*

CONTENTS

Basil   1

ONE

Guide to Greece   5
Ambassador of the Dead   6
Singing Contests   9
Odysseus Seeing Laertes   11
Heads of the Hydra   12
Filo   14
Source of the Styx   15
Name Day   17
A Fragment from Three Secret Poems   19

TWO

The Deaf-Blind Girl   23
Language and Darkness   25
Thebes   27
Choreography   28
Sitari   29
Ataraxia   30

THREE

Emma   35
Pulp Fiction   37
Panopeus   38
Thelpousa   39
Poseidonians   41
Poseidonians II   42
Jackie O Dead   43
Home from Greece   45
Tour Guide for the Romans   47

The Philippeum (168 B.C.E.)   48

Arsinoë   49

Ancient Athens on PBS   50

FOUR

Hermes   55

The Scholars Critique Pausanias' Style   63

Idiot Savant   65

Gorgon   66

Achilles in the Underworld   67

FIVE

On Sir James Frazer's Note to the Catalogue of Old Trees in
   Pausanias   71

Stefana   73

Relative   75

Iconostasis   76

Athanasios   77

Austerity Measures I   79

Austerity Measures II   80

SIX

Clearing my Throat   85

Olympian 14   86

Agganis   88

Pausanias at the Tomb of Hyacinth   91

On the Deck of a Ship   92

Argonauts   93

The Rowers   95

Lament for the Makers   96

SEVEN

Tibullus in Sparta   101

Somewhere Outside Mosul   102

Easter in the Oven   103

Hellmouth   104

Mycenae: Pausanias Conducts a Guided Tour of the Burial
    Chambers   106

Arlington National Cemetery   108

Omens   109

Sailing to Byzantium   111

Minerva Tritonia   112

EIGHT

Origins   117

Grackle   118

Palimpsest   119

Andidoro   121

Reciprocity   122

Cricket Song   124

Franklin Park Zoo   125

Peregrinations of Pausanias   127

Acknowledgments   131

Notes   133

GUIDE
TO GREECE

BASIL

Sometimes on Sundays, while we were still asleep,
My father blessed the house with a basil leaf
And a little glass half-filled with holy water.
The sprig was from our next-door neighbor's garden.

And the holy water seemed no different to us
Than faucet water, although it came from church,
In clear plastic tubes that looked like medicine bottles
When they were filled with light on the kitchen sill.

Most times I'd wake up just in time to see him
Pass down the hall, dipping the sprig in a glass
As he sprinkled every doorway in the house,
Repeating something in Greek I couldn't follow—

Some phrase he muttered quickly under his breath
Each time the sprig would break the water's surface:
And then I was seeing through a glass so clearly
Even the veins of the leaf stood out from a distance.

Before I knew it the whole house smelled of basil.
You could count your blessings in the sunlit dew
Cast off so lightly, but never nonchalantly,
By the leaf in his right hand; as if you were struck

By the morning glimmer left on everything
The water happened to touch, drawing a bead
On the dilating bead that brightened the bureau's brass handle,
And kept you focused on the here and now.

Until a later date, when the priest would perform
The very same ritual all over again—
But this time stopping at the threshold of
The altar, where the sleeper refused to wake.

Do we call the glass half-empty, or is it half-full?
The answering voice breaks off between the verses:
Βασιλικό. My tongue curls back on its stem
Like a wet leaf, companion to low chanting.

ONE

GUIDE TO GREECE

Endless genealogies, as densely entangled
As a grove of olive trees, his grasp of their roots

Extending all the way back to Epaminondas,
Who sprang from the earth of Thebes, before it was Thebes;

Cities erected on sites of ruined cities,
Their marble temples and strange foundation myths;

Baedeker to Bassae, Athens, Delphi,
For Roman tourists of the *Pax Romana;*

And if this means, Pausanias, that no one
Knows better than you that everything that's happened

Has already happened before, and also because
Both Sparta and Arcadia are places

You call *Archaía Elláda,* and that's a term
I heard my parents use to tell us where

They came from when they meant to say *Old Greece,*
I keep on reading down all the lists of names,

Pausanias, keep paging through each region
And wondering if perhaps you might have seen them,

My elderly parents, somewhere in your travels.

AMBASSADOR OF THE DEAD

My parents were never crazy about Cavafy—
They didn't know much about poetry, at all,
And barely had time to read anything but the papers;

Though sometimes a poem they liked would appear in their
Beloved *Hellenic Voice*. (A poem that was always
In rhyming stanzas, and deeply nostalgic.) Or else

I'd show them one of the Modern Greek poets that I
Was trying to translate, and ask for their advice
About a line. "Is this for school?" they'd say.

My parents were never crazy about Cavafy—
To them he was too refined, too ALEX-AN-
DRIAN, and they were only peasants, *khoriátes*.

And there was no Ithaka for them to go back to.
When I'd beg them to read the Greek, they'd balk when they got
To his purist *katharévousa* diction—they just

Couldn't stomach its formalist starch. His poems were never
Demotic enough, never *trapézika:*
Songs to be sung across the kitchen table.

And if I read them Elytis, Odysseus Elytis
Too was too elitist to trust, too drunk
On the island sun of his own Ionian vision

To people for whom elevation meant being raised
In the steepening shadows of Peloponnesos.
("The great Odysseus," my father would chide.)

And if Yannis Ritsos spoke their working-class language,
And his poems weren't hard to follow, still, once they heard
That Ritsos was Marxist that's all they needed to know.

But read us some more Seferi, I hear them say,
As I sit and write at a green Formica table,
The same one where we sat together and ate

In another century. Was it Mandelstam
Who said that poetry, to him, was bread
From the kitchen table, but that his words were dead

If he tried to start a poem by looking up
At the stars? Osip Mandelstam, who wrote:
The evening stars against the horizon glistened

Like salt on the blade of an axe. I think my parents
Would've liked that verse, and called it *trapézika.*
Saying that, their shades appear in the table's reflection,

Looking up as if they were thirsting for something to drink.
Read us some more Seferi. Noblesse oblige
Seferiádes, that haughty diplomat who,

In his British banker's suits, had seen the world.
French Symbolist figs and Earl Grey with Eliot.
And stones too heavy to lift without his learning.

But also deep silence as old Europe explodes.
And crowded refugee ships as a form of transport.
Ambassador of the high Modernist, ancient Dead.

Read us that one about Stratís, you know, Stratís
Thalassinós, I hear my parents intone,
Their voices, as soft as the hiss of the surf in Seferis,

Calling from the floor of the Dead Sea, though the smooth
Formica shines green as the placid Aegean of poems.
And then my mother returns to her ironing board,

The steam-iron dipping like a prow that's driving
Through choppy waves, the pile of freshly laundered
Butcher's aprons as white as white-washed Piraeus.

And now my father's back at his block, still reading
The smoking entrails. He has turned the victim's head
So its eyes are facing Erebos. Or Smyrna.

I'm spreading handfuls of sawdust, and watching it soak up the blood.

SINGING CONTESTS

I

That the judges may be deaf is not unheard of.
Was it Enfield, forsaken parish, whose poetry prize
Conferred on Keats an *honorable mention*?

And then there's "A Tuft of Flowers," that early beauty
By Frost, unchanged from his undergraduate days—
A poem once marked B+ by a Harvard prof.

But when it comes to hearing, no one gets it
Right all the time, not even on Parnassus,
Where there's a village that calls its singing contest

"The best in the world." Lofty, small-town pride.
It was Orpheus himself Pausanias says
The shepherds say took part in their competition,

Looking like golden Apollo with his lyre.
But Orpheus left in a huff, and never turned back
When they said: *Too full of himself. Second place.*

And Marsyas, poor soul, whose flesh the god would flay,
Kept hitting his high note until he was blue in the face.
Even Homer was sent back home a loser—and if

We're tactfully not told why, village rumor
Had it the bard they called *The Voice* went on
For way too long. But Hesiod's rustic songs

From *Works and Days* were a hit with those mountain folk;
Still, Hesiod didn't know how to play the lyre
While he was singing, and this disqualified him.

Pausanias notes the legend of the winners'
Names he saw engraved around and around
A bronze cauldron, but doesn't make any comment.

Names not even vaguely familiar now:
Echembrotos, Melampous, Eleuther, Philammon . . .
Like reading down the names from those yellowed, stacked-up

Volumes of *The Dial*, or *Poetry*.

II

In Ákovos, my father's village, I saw
The festival they call the *Panigýrie*.
Arcadian shepherds singing in competition

On a makeshift stage completely in the dark.
From the back of a pickup truck a spotlight pointed
Up at the shaggy peak the singers faced.

Somewhere Pausanias says that Pindar's songs
Were played by Pan himself, but that the local
Shepherds he heard recite them were unconvincing.

Really? All night we heard demotic song,
Our faces lit by amber shots of *rakí*
That must have been at least a hundred proof.

All night the voices of Kouna, Manóli, Stratís—
Not sweet Menálcus and Lycidas. All night
The shaggy beard of the cliff was glistening.

ODYSSEUS SEEING LAERTES

It's getting dark, and he's still in the yard. By now
She'd be stewing over the steamy *katsaróles*
She has to reheat, but glad that he's finally home.

He's inspecting his favorite tree, the sour quince.
All day he's been hacking away at carcasses
Of frozen chickens, piled up on his chopping block

Like little hecatombs of smoking entrails.
The sour quince has put forth pink and white petals,
Like the flakes of sawdust stuck to his blood-stained work-boots.

As when I was a boy, standing away from the shade,
And he would turn and see me, and call me over,
Singing, from the trees, that line from the swallow song:

Come here, little bird. Come here, come here, don't go.

HEADS OF THE HYDRA

Pausanias thinks the Hydra had only one head—
Like those other vipers and snakes infesting these swamps.

But in his *Theogony,* Hesiod says the Hydra,
Like the hellish bitch it sprang from, had *fifty* heads,

And each one spontaneously regenerative—
Till Hercules severed them all, and, thinking he killed it,

Dipped the barbs of his arrows in venomous gall
As black as the ooze of these Lernaean lagoons.

"The Hydra was reared by gentle Amymone's spring,"
The villagers sing to the gushing water they call

"The Blameless One." But who was that later poet
Who numbered Hercules' labors? Obscure as his haunted,

Persistent dread of impending catastrophe,
He multiplied the heads of the Hydra in heightened,

Interminably long surreally unfurling
Hexameter lines—however toothless his couplets.

Like that horror film for a rainy day in July,
When the marquee promised a matinee hothouse of grisly,

Neon exfoliation: *Day of the Triffids.*
In Kincaid's theater, transfixed by man-eating plants

And jittery newsreels of jungles in Vietnam,
The self-elongating beam projected a tentacle

Of teeming dust above our impressionable heads.
On the other hand, *On the Natural History of*

Destruction, the shade of Sebald, in the shade
Of Goethe's oak, in the shadow of Buchenwald,

In block after block of page-long paragraphs
Insisting upon exact, first-hand transcription,

As in Dr. Hachiya's *Hiroshima Diary;*
As in that flat description of strobe-lit Leipzig

That Sebald heard from his mother, and how, to the child,
The dark was a sky on fire, and he learned to equate

The word for *rubble* with the word for *city.*
And it was Iolas, young servant of Hercules,

Who torched the stumps' decapitated black roots
Until those writhing, elongated trunks were ash.

(And this was done, says Hesiod, *just in case.*)
Long after the hero had severed the Hydra's heads,

The strafing continued. The bombers headed for Dresden,
Destroying the Gothic church and the fire hoses.

FILO

It's when you forgot, and the oven caught on fire—
Serious enough to require extinguishers—
Your baking days, we knew, were finally done.
The golden joy of making gone black as that.

That all came back on cleaning out a cupboard
Lined with contact paper, and finding, beyond
The electric mixer's poised aluminum spindles,
That drab gray tin you kept your recipes in.

Written in ballpoint pen, on 3×5 cards.
Ancient archive, meticulous enough
For a town library, circa nineteen sixty.
Like filo dough the cards were furled at the edges.

On a few, the faintest vestige of baking powder
Still ghosted their exacting measurements.
Just one, judging by its sticky yellowed
Thumbprint, had honey's stamp of sublime approval.

By the deliquescing light of the kitchen window
I savored each polysyllabic elaboration
Of your most intricate, richly layered confections:
Galaktoboúriko, Baklava, Kataífi . . .

And there you are, your lowered face aglow
By the oven's open door, back when that glazed,
Oblivious look spelled something like rapture—not
A recipe for imminent disaster.

Galaktoboúriko, Baklava, Kataífi . . .
Those honeyed hot-out-of-the-oven terms of the Greek.
My index of an art so light it must
Have felt like nothing on its silver tray.

SOURCE OF THE STYX

Polygnotos painted the gurgling pit of blood
And over it a crouching Odysseus—
Back on his heels before the abrupt abyss.
I saw it in Phokis: the shades of the underworld,

Depicted on muraled walls not far from Delphi.
The prophet Teiresias, first to rise from the pit,
Comes walking towards you, silently tapping his staff
On the darkness before him—a blind man crossing the street.

And there, in the gloom, oblivious to her son's
Dilemma, Antikleia stares and drools.
Elpenor wraps himself up in an army blanket.
And further down, their feet cut off by the frame,

Perithous and Theseus sit on marble thrones.
Glaze-eyed they gaze at their gleaming swords, holding
Them out in their outstretched hands as if their two-edged
Blades were useless down there, still thirsting for blood.

Those smooth-limbed princes, ensconced in the mural's stone.
I saw it in Phokis, and see it in darkness now,
If memory serves, oblivion's jet-black water
Suffusing these Stygian crags: *Mavroneró*—

Which might be the same that Hölderlin beheld
As a level stream of human faces pouring
Over the ledge of remembrance, steeped as he was
In that dense, unstanched procession. *Mavroneró:*

Phantasmal pulse and flow: as if my blood
Was thirsting to speak in the torrent's babbling tongue:
"Kill me in the light," Ajax prays to himself,
Dardanians swarming around him, the one whose shield

Was known as The Wall, engulfed by a storm of dust;
"The City fell," said the note that was tied to a bird;
"Oh help us, please," they call so late at night,
From the nursing home or *the blackened ridge of Psará*.

NAME DAY

We've heard it before, and it's still the same old story
Now that you're eighty, that one about the baptism,

When nobody knew what the baby's name would be—
Not even your parents, standing so close to the tremulous

Mouth of the marble font—until the godparents,
Mr. and Mrs. Bozas, had made their choice,

And whispered it to the priest. Then the naked infant
Is lowered into the tub of oily water.

We've heard it before, but the water doesn't brim
Until you call the font a *kolymbíthra*,

And then I see the streaming infant emerge
From a radiant pool of sound, kicking and screaming

As if it were born again from the sheer pleasure
You take in saying a word like *kolymbíthra*.

We've heard it before, which means that even before
The ceremony is over, you're already out

The door of the Orthodox Church in Old New Bedford,
Running down Myrtle Street on a bright spring day,

Because you're the oldest child, and it's your job
To tell the missing elders the name of the newborn,

For which they'll thank you with a little change—
Coins no brighter than the ring of the name

You carried back on your tongue. We've heard it before,
The one about the river of oblivion,

Whose brackish water we taste before we're born.
But that's another story. Your youngest sister

Is wrapped like a mummy, and we're still waiting to hear
Her name from you, holding our breath for a sign

Of *Leucotheia* lifted from the water.

A FRAGMENT FROM THREE SECRET POEMS

—Seferis

I can't remember which murky river it was
That carried us away. We sank like stones.
Now the rush of the current is over our heads,
And the swaying reeds on the water are writing something
None of us could fathom.

TWO

THE DEAF-BLIND GIRL

A handbook for the soul no one can read.
A vale that's watered by tears. A private school
For deaf-blind children, in Brookline, where I worked,

Part-time, with a little girl in constant agony,
Profoundly autistic, the one we called *Antigone*.
She always wore a helmet, even while sleeping,

Because, as an infant, she'd blinded herself with her fists.
An orange, perforated, styrofoam helmet
To ward off the sleepless demons inside her head.

(It's one thing to sing the form the frightened hare
Once left in the melting snow, another to wince
At a harelip whose trembling cleft will never depart.)

If she wasn't held, or strapped to a chair with restraints,
She'd batter her eyes and ears, her nose and mouth,
As if she were trying to shut down all of her senses.

Little Antigone, buried alive in herself.
(O healing god of dreams, Asclepian snake,
Your cure the spell that enters through our ears:

Could you not slither through those cauliflowers?)
She signed with her hands, but only when prompted by staff.
And then always the same three frantic gesticulations

For Eat, and Drink, and More—as if anorexic
Language could only express the naked hunger
It cannot feed, as it screamed through the tongues in her hands

For Eat and Drink and More. And yet, at the sink,
With her tiny fists still clenched, she would stand calm
For a couple of hours, as the steady warm stream kept pouring

Down over her hands, until like flower buds
Her tiny fists unfurled to the faucet water.
Now the gush of it splashed against her outstretched palms—

Ecstatic stigmata—as she alternated her hands,
One over the other, as though in eloquent discourse
With the one who quenched her thirst, the Anne Sullivan

Of the shining, babbling water, the water that held her
As warm as the womb of never being born.
Her frizzy, unhelmeted hair. The faucet unfailing.

Her eyes that were never open, except at the sink.
Her pupils like gray-blue fuses of broken bulbs.
That spellbound little girl, at home in the school

For the deaf and blind, just standing there by a pair
Of gleaming knobs and the fluent, effusive water—
And looking as if she'd solved the Sphinx's riddle.

LANGUAGE AND DARKNESS

As dark as it is outside tonight, as dark
As the haunted wood inside, as black as those spaces
Between the stars—light shines on a thrush's breast,
Singing in its sleep from desert places.

Reading Radnoti's eclogue, the one he scrawled
In the searchlight dark of a Nazi labor camp—
Though not so dark that we can't pick up the gleam
Of an earthworm's slime, as the line goes squiggling blind.

In sicknesse and in sinne, George Herbert cried,
Believing in affliction's Easter Wings,
Though it was Poetry that furthered the flight
Of the book he asked *dear brother Ferrar* to burn.

Lovely enchanting language, sugar-cane,
Hony of roses, whither wilt thou flie?
From this broken flesh we fly, Radnóti replies,
But only if reverie's key still turns in its lock.

Paralyzed almost a decade by ALS—
Unspeakable, yes, but my friend George Mazaréas
Speaks to his wife and young daughter by blinking slowly:
Spelling the words they read aloud from his eyes.

And if they lose track of the letters, arranged in rows
On a numbered mental grid—mortification.
The blinking stops, like taps from the walls of a cell.
Their voices go mute as the tube attached to his throat.

And now the Haitian nurse Elijah kneels
Beside the wheelchair. The wingéd word arrives
In the blink of an eye—but not until Elijah
Speaks, by the gleaming spokes of a chariot wheel.

When she'd refused a second glass of wine,
Cynthia's husband, bound to his chair, began
Intently blinking his eyes. D-O-N'-T W-O-R-R-Y, H-O-N-E-Y.
I C-A-N D-R-I-V-E. His jaw strapped shut, but his biting,

Rueful humor still champing at the bit.
Call it the self *in extremis* expressing itself,
It's George's way of spelling out who he is
By telling us his gallant sick joke at the party.

Tony Judt, composing his final essays
Late at night, still wide awake to the words.
Unable to scratch an itch, or change his position,
He writes in his head—*but not in the dark,* he said.

Lying in that excruciating bed.

THEBES

Porphyry says propitiate the gods
Of Mount Olympus with snow-white altars, for Hades

Keep the voracious chthonic hearths well-fed.
But here in Thebes, please tell us, Porphyry, why

All night Apollo's altar is left unlit,
The charred remains remain unstirred. As if only

The sparkless ashes can speak to the blackest hours
In terms that kindle nothing. O golden Apollo,

How dark the darkest pyre snuffs out the day,
The day piled high with the depositions of night:

Terra cotta griffins, tiny bronze tripods,
Necklaces, rings, crutches, clasps, nails, cups . . .

Hooded by a towel, I bow my congested head
To a pan of boiling water, inhaling the healing

Fumes still rising up from the days when I
Was acolyte of the eucalyptus leaf,

And no one I knew had yet become a shade.
But here in Thebes, no sacred groves—although

Like votive scrolls the foliage unfurls,
Wherein each tremulous medicinal fern

The light appears to pool, like honey poured in a spoon.

CHOREOGRAPHY

Mousikí. Dark stacks of scratchy records
Free-falling in time. A Magnavox needle so giddy
It skipped right off the vinyl. Though not before

The groove it cut had left its trace, your songs
Unscathed as the Memorex disks that play them now—
Those shrill folk-ballad refrains, that keep coming back,

Like the scratchy voice of a needle lost in a haystack.
Sunk back so far in the sofa cushions, your feet
Are dancing on air, not knowing where you are

Though it's the same parlor where you taught me the steps
Of the circle dances, leading me by the hand
Around the coffee table. Most days you can't

Remember your name, but once the music starts
You close your eyes, and call out what goes with each song,
Those dances that never leave you in the dark:

Zeibékiko, Tsámiko, Syrtó, Kalamátianó . . .
The plush of the parlor carpet softened my first,
Hesitant steps out of boyhood. No wobblier than

The wobbling pivot of those sun-warped LPs,
Undulating in mesmerizing waves
On the velvet stand revolving under them

As smoothly as Homer's simile still turns
The dancing-floor of Daedalus to a wheel
Caressed in the potter's hands. And that's how they danced,

Engraved on the shield by the hobbled god, Hephaestus.
Demented, vertiginous music. No turning spindle
Whose spooling thread the labyrinth can't unravel.

"Maybe, if you learn these steps, you'll marry a Greek girl."

SITARI

Right after the funerals, and forty days later,
Sitári was served with fish, downstairs from church,
Where it was waiting for us in paper cups.

Tiny white cups like the kind for ketchup and relish
Or filled with all sorts of pills on the shiny tray
In Papou's hospital room. Sugar-coated bits

Of boiled wheat that had to be eaten first
When somebody died—back when that somebody
Was always some elderly, distant relation from Greece.

Back when each grain, or so the priest would say,
"Was one of your sins," which was all he had to say
For each kernel's dark gleam to shine through the saccharine.

Sitári. You fork it up gingerly now, now that
So many are gone from those gatherings, and find it
As densely packed and as deeply ingrained as ever.

The seed that fell to the ground, and died; and the seed
That was saved, with its ashen look of wind-blown chaff—
The nub of the parable still a harrowed mouthful.

Call it immigrant caviar, served up
By a scythe and an elderly aunt in a long black shawl.
Sitári. A thimbleful of the stubble fields

I can almost taste. Winnowed stalks that speak
To me through a clustered, sibilant rustle. Wild spores
Of my diaspora caught on the prongs of a fork.

More baleful gleams from the marble threshing floors.

ATARAXIA

My eyes don't seal when I sleep, which means they never
Close, all the way, at night. It's been that way

For me since childhood—trying to keep the dark
Away by keeping an eye on it, while I sleep,

Half-awake, like a zombie. *Exposure Keratopathy.*
Severe dry eyes. Nothing to worry about,

Asclepius assures me, as long as those tiny,
Crosshatching scars remain on the vitreous humor,

The whites of each eyeball—which is a fairly benign
Tearless sign of merciless deformity

Scratching its way towards the oblivious corneas.
Last night I read Keats, Keats who read Chapman all night,

Until Homer's blind vision dawned on him, and seeing
A whole new planet swim into his Greekless ken,

He wrote that sonnet. Asclepius prescribes
All kinds of daily salves, but no lasting balm,

And sleeping goggles, whose lenses are black as night—
Not Tranquil Eyes, but what he likes to call

Ataraxia's Mask: a black silk scrim
So dark it soothes by its sheer opacity,

And helps me dream of nothing—the only cure,
Asclepius says, Ataraxia's Mask.

Every night I strap it on over my eyes,
To keep the lids moist by keeping them glued to their tears.

Impenetrable pads of spongy webbing.
I stare into clumps of moss as thick and black

As the hellebore of hell, on Lethe's banks.
One morning I won't be able to tear them off.

Tonight I read Keats, sumptuous, vivid Keats,
But couldn't get past the rococo stuff of his dreams,

Woven from reams of Flemish tapestry:
The carvéd angels, ever-eager eyed,

Star'd, where upon their heads the cornice rests
With hair blown back, and wings . . . I closed the book.

A tiny seamstress is sewing my eyelids shut.

THREE

EMMA

Náhabédian. The sound of the name still clicks
Like a string of worry beads that keeps coming back
Around to the glassy look of our next-door neighbor:
That reclusive, elderly lady from Armenia.

But in our language *Emma* also meant blood,
And we felt a certain bond with her whenever
We caught a lingering whiff of some spicy aroma
Wafted through her kitchen curtains, or heard

So faintly the long shrill cry of a clarinet solo
Playing somewhere inside, on scratchy records.
But unlike us, there were never any relatives
Going in and out of her house, even on Sundays.

Before I knew what happened to her family
I knew it had something to do with those heavy rugs
She draped across her porch, and the motes of dust
She would beat from them with a broom, until the rich

Embroidery was beaten back to colors
Whose blaze the autumn leaves could only dream of.
And once, when my mother was sick with a cold, or the flu,
And we needed some sprigs of mint from Emma's garden

To season the roasting lamb, I was sent next door
With a dish of pastry. All I would ever know
About the brittleness of any brightness
Was there in those little golden confected scrolls

Of honeyed filo that felt so light in my hands.
Díples we called them. And if they started out
As shapeless lumps of dough, that only made me
More impressionable as I watched the work

Of fingers encrusted like a potter's. And if
Those *díples* were always sealed in cellophane wrap,
Then stored in the parlor dark, that helps me recall
Their luster more clearly, and lets me assess it more coolly.

Even though I knew nothing at all about Virgil
And those sweets he says the Sybil used as treats
To silence the triple mouths of Cerberus,
I knew Emma heard barking from the gates of Hell.

Maybe it's only because she'd never seen me
Up close, or maybe the morning mist was coming
Off the ocean (back when the whole Atlantic
Was down the street), but something seemed to lift

Where Emma knelt, and made her eyes water
As I stepped through the fog—though it wasn't me
She saw that day, but a boy who was just my age.
In the garden, holding out the honeycombs.

PULP FICTION

Roubánis. Just writing his name is enough for me
To hear my mother's voice, and how she would say
It sounded so melancholy—meaning that song
He played on the church organ. Some haunting tune

He was always obsessing over, right up until
It was time for choir practice. That was the year
Their choir master was haughty, distracted Roubánis:
Itinerant artist with the exotic, and slightly

Ridiculous sounding, Middle Eastern name.
And what was she supposed to know about
Rembétika—moody Greek taverna music
From Anatolia—she, a teenage girl

Just coming of age in nineteen thirties New Bedford?
All she knew was what her parents told her,
Knew that the name of the song was *Misirlou,*
And it sounded so melancholy—especially there,

In that drafty little church with the empty pews.
And then she'd go and put on the record, the record
Roubánis made. That song that came from our parlor,
Back when the couches were covered with plastic sheets.

And now I can't believe it's *Misirlou*
I'm hearing as background music in a film
By Quentin Tarantino—but there it is,
As Oriental as ever. Indrawn and slow.

Overblown as the maestro's nom de plume
Unfurling like smoke from a Turkish water pipe.
Surreal as a squeezed syringe filling up with blood,
Or those parlor couches covered with plastic sheets.

PANOPEUS

Stop at the city of Panopeus. That is,
If it can be called a city, given it has
No center, no government buildings, no amphitheater,
And no gymnasium; no open market
With stalls for Sophists' debates and tremulous scales
For haggling over the sudden dip in the drachma;
No libraries; no leaping public fountains
Where flawless nudes embrace under arching dolphins
Whose fluent mouths recirculate the foam.

Stop at Panopeus. Look hard at it:
That city where the Phokian people keep
To themselves, on steep ravines, with their monasteries
And mish-mash mud-hovels. Their nameless headstones askew,
Each rough-hewn slab inscribed with a line of scripture
Cut into rock as obdurate as the fields
They tend. By frozen streams that never gush.
Something from the Psalms, as clear as the *Koine*
Greek into which it's carved. And simple as *Lo,*

I am with you, unto the end of Time.

THELPOUSA

The gods, they claim, gave them the identical choice.
But unlike Athens, the people of Thelpousa
Preferred the sea-god's steeds to Athena's gift.

The pent-up Thelpousans chose the glossy stallions
Champing at wild Poseidon's foaming bit
Instead of *eliés:* those olive eyes that gleam

From the dry (but salubrious) leaves of Wisdom's tree.
Look! they said. *It's the blood of the god with his lapis
Lazuli mane that surges up from the rocks—*

Though I saw only a leaping, ebullient fountain.
Landlocked impulsive Thelpousa picked unbridled
Poseidon instead of Athena. Hence, no Socrates,

Plato, Thucydides, Solon, Hippocrates, Euclid . . .
No Parthenon friezes of flowing stately procession,
Just tiny bent figures trudging along the ridge.

No Gettysburg, no oratory. And nothing
To gloss in the *Blue Guide to Pericles' Greece.* But plenty
Of slate-gray hillocks to serve as unmarked landmarks.

No oedipal introspection. Just unchecked, nascent,
Indelible waves of dysfunction, vaguely diffused.
Incandescent Electra, raging offstage.

No lucrative gloom of the silver mines, up north,
With slaves under twelve to fit the twelve-inch shafts
From which they emerge, as black as chimney sweeps.

Instead of the rooted olive, unruly waves.
Instead of the flaring nostrils of F-16s,
Or the polypragmatic wink on the painted prows

Of imperial triremes, Polish cavalry charges.
The people of Thelpousa. We used to call them
Company, when they came to visit on Sunday,

Their voices still boisterous, late, in the living room.
Now here they are in an ancient homemade movie
From the sixties, back in their backwater, mountain-peak town.

They're sitting around a table that's set for a feast,
Conversing intently about something that makes them grimace,
Then flail away with gestures. *O shuddering reel*

Of laughing shades, you with your heads thrown back
And your mouths still chewing, holding up half-empty glasses
To the camera panning your hapless, ingenuous faces:

As vivid as life itself, without any sound.

POSEIDONIANS

—Cavafy

After so many years of commingling with
Tyrrenhians, Latins, and other foreigners,
The Poseidonians forgot the Greek language.
All their ancestral ways had faded away—
Except for a beautiful Greek festival
With lyres and flutes, and contests for laurel wreaths.

And every year, as the festival drew to a close,
They would wonder aloud about their ancient Greek names,
And try them out on each other—at least those few
Who still knew the sound of their Poseidonian names.
So their festival, when all was said and done,
Would always conclude on a melancholy note.

At the end of the day, they too were Greeks—but only
So long as their annual ritual made them remember
That they were citizens, once, of *Magna Graecia*.
But now they had to face how far they'd fallen,
Speaking and acting like those they used to call
Barbarians. Cut off, alas, from *Hellás*.

POSEIDONIANS II

What all the maps now call *Salonika*
Was once the ancient city of *Poseidonias:*
Named for settlers who came in the vanishing wake
Of their leader, a hunter who swam the open seas,
Pursuing a deer, and lost track of it there, the headlands
He named for his people adrift. And later the same

Meandering tribe will land in *Magna Graecia;*
And later still lament the Greek they can't speak,
In the great Alexandrian's poem about amnesia
Confounding the annual festival. Was it purely
Coincidence that their royal stock, Cavafy,
Goes back to a king whose murky origin,

As far as we know, appears to be Egyptian?
Can the irony that's deep in a poet's bloodlines
Be traced, like a name, through Ancestry.com?
But the deer-in-the-headlights look belongs to my parents,
In an open field in Ipswich, when all the tents
At the church picnic go dark, and we search for our car.

JACKIE O DEAD

—*London Times* headline

My parents abhorred the great Jackie O
For marrying Onassis. "That widow's

A curse," my mother hissed. "Just wait
And see. And she's not *that* pretty. Not

Like Athena"—meaning the blond, Greek ex.
And next it's my father's laconic kvetch:

"His business went bad. The cancer spread.
His only son, Alexandros, dead."

My parents never called him "filthy rich."
But *O Kaïménos,* the Pitiful Wretch.

And from the way they said it to us,
You'd think Onassis was Oedipus.

Big oil. The glut of conglomerates.
To my Marxist Uncle Leonidas

It was all a western conspiracy:
No uncouth Greek could rule the sea.

It all came back in that full page headline
I saw one rainy day in London.

The sandwich-board draped in plastic: *JACKIE
O DEAD.* Her favorite poet Cavafy.

The streaks of rain pelting the sheet . . .
Of cellophane that keeps the yacht

Scotch-taped to the door of our Fridgidaire
Pristine. That's Churchill, slumped in a deck chair.

He looks out across the sunlit Aegean
Straight into our sallow linoleum kitchen.

My mother's shade, still adamant
We're somehow related to Maria

Callas, whose name was no different
Than ours—until she changed it, *that Diva.*

HOME FROM GREECE

—Cavafy

So here we are, Hermippos, almost there—
And the captain has confirmed it. I believe he said
The day after tomorrow. But even so,
At least we're sailing across our own waters now,
Carried along by those familiar currents,
The ones that take us back to our own countries:
Cyprus, Syria, Egypt. But why so quiet,
Hermippos? Aren't we both in the very same boat,
Feeling happier the farther from Greece we go?
We really should stop fooling ourselves. And isn't
That just what it means to be Greek, if you ask your heart?

It's time we acknowledged the truth: we too are Greeks.
(What else could we be?) But drawn to things and moved
In ways that to other Hellenes can seem so strange
Our Greekness might as well be another world—
One that goes all the way back to its Asian roots.

Just think how unbecoming of us it would be,
As philosophers, if we chose to speak in some phony
Athenian accent, like those petty provincial kings
With their pompous (and of course "Macedonian") titles.
Remember how ludicrous they appeared to us
Whenever they happened to show up at our lectures?
No matter how hard they tried to keep it veiled,
Somehow a bit of Arabia, or even Persia,
Was always showing through. And how they tried
To hide the slightest *faux pas,* those poor wretches,
Concocting some pathetic ostentation.

No, that's not our style at all. For Greeks like us,
That kind of pettiness never measures up.

So what if the blood that's flowing through our veins
Just happens to be Syrian, or Egyptian?
That's nothing to be ashamed of. But all the more reason,
Hermippos, that we should know how to honor it.

TOUR GUIDE FOR THE ROMANS

Two decades of foot-slog. One pack-mule for the peaks.
And you, like Aesop's tortoise, just plodding along,

Pausanias. Jack-rabbit heart with no spring in your step.
The whole of Hellas a mountainous shell of itself.

Inviolate ruins. And Greece in the smarmy palms
Of garrulous dealers posterity will treasure.

They'll leave no stone unturned. For what it's worth
You set it down in code: those broken inscriptions

Transcribed to keep the sanctuaries hidden
Within some inscrutable, inner recess of language.

Both the *bizarrerie* and the brilliance met
With a blank expression: preserving for the vatic

Present the vacant look of proleptic loss.
Pax Romana. Pox Macedonia, *pace*

The sun beating down on the ridge of your pulsing skull.
The unremitting altars. Old blood on the dogmas.

Between the village of Strangled Artemis
And the grove of Hanged Helen, that shrine where Eros

Is older than his mother, though still a child.
He hovers above the foam as if it were slime.

His tomb's encrusted with coral and narwhal horns.
And later, all kinds of overgrown marginalia.

Further north, the coast of Thessaly. With snow
On its shoulder. Wild *Thálassa's* turn to bear the world.

THE PHILIPPEUM (168 B.C.E.)

Serene the seven Ionic pillars, perfect
The circle of elegant closure. Cerulean
The glazed rotunda, whose apex is circumscribed
By a bronze, funereal poppy. Purple the clusters
On terraced slopes beyond the treasury building
Annexing the shrine, at the foot of Chronios.
On sanctified grounds of the holy chthonic mother.

The Macedonians still occupy
The inner sanctum, the Romans are on their way.
Shoulder to shoulder stand Philip and Alexander.
And Philip's parents, Eurydice and Amyntas,
Sit with his wife; but Philip's divorced first wife,
Olympias, doting mother of Alexander,
Is also present—which means Leochares, the Master

Sculptor, was ordered to add her figure: hence
The tense, domestic-dynastic, convivial scene
Before the Great one finally left for Asia,
Before those commissions for *flawless Grecian copies*
In gold and ivory, by the neorealist
School of Leochares, in the catastrophic
Aftermath of Chaironeia, now Pydna.

ARSINOË

Ptolemy II, who failed to stop Macedonia,
Is *Philadelphos,* who murdered two of his brothers
And warred against Magas, his rebellious half-brother.
He married his sister Arsinoë. The Ptolemies say
They inherited their Egyptian polygyny
From Philip II, the great Alexander's father.
On Helikon Pausanias saw a frieze:
Arsínoë astride a bronze ostrich. The girl
Unable to bear, the grounded wings outstretched.
Philadelphos, friend of the "late" Greek poets.
Followed by the sacker of Thebes, *Philo-*
Mater, at war with his mother. *Ptolemaic*
Kindnesses too many to list, the doomed
Athenians carved on his statue, bronze arm in arm
With Berenike, his only legitimate child.

ANCIENT ATHENS ON PBS

Finally home for a weekend. But when I enter,
Silence. My mother hardly looks up from the TV.
Sitting in the kitchen, transfixed before our Zenith.

For once the screen's pristine. No static. No snow.
No fussing with the antenna, frantic to stop
The picture's waterfall of unreeling frames.

None of that at all. Just zoned-out focus,
Unfazed that the fizz in her ginger ale is flat.
Or that the teetering stack of Triscuits remains

Untouched in its pewter dish. Then an ad comes on.
She wipes away tears. "So beautiful, O this show . . .
They showed the urns . . . And the people with their pebbles.

The people putting their pebbles into the urns . . .
Into one, or the other one . . . That's how it started.
Demokratía. You know? *Katalavaíneis?*"

I'm studying classics with William Arrowsmith
And Donald S. Carne-Ross. Euripides
And Sophocles. I sit. And watch the show.

Later that night, just after Peter Jennings,
Her dentures go into a glass of soda water.
And they don't come out again until the news

From another century keeps mouthing the D word
So much I hardly know what it means anymore,
Bandied about in the name of brutal aggression—

Just as it was in the time of Thucydides.
But my mother's shade is oblivious to the ironic.
She clacks her guileless gums in genuine awe:

"*Demokratía.* You know? *Katalavaíneis?*"
And as the crumbs of the crackers crystallize,
Like specimen cultures in a petri dish,

She's still in her dusting apron, glued to the set.

FOUR

HERMES

Add your stone to the turtle's cairn

Trikrena's fountains are only a trickle now,
Though once three nymphs came rushing down the valley
To lave the infant Hermes, thinking the blood

They washed was his mother's blood, not the birth of music.
Like baby Krishna, they found him eating the dirt,
In order to get the taste of the world on his tongue—

The taste of ashes that comes with the messenger god.
It was one of the mountain turtles sacred to Pan
The infant Hermes, precocious (already a thief),

Eviscerated, and strung with a rabbit's guts.
Trikrena, sacred rills of the Trickster's wiles.
Psychopomp of the crossroads, and stone phallus.

Even the Olympians couldn't ostracize him.

Oud

Coils of cuneiform script rewound on a narrow scroll,
Or the view from a garden wall with a trellis of razor wire.

Intrinsic fretwork, out of western earshot. Oud.
Its crescent moon as silky smooth as a trackless dune.

Wind-strummed grasses fanning out before the choppers.
A mouthful of streaming hair and a crick in the ostrich neck.

Ingrained moods of the hallowed bole sealed off with black pitch.
Until the music extrudes, like myrrh from the cedar groves.

The head of Orpheus cradled like a watermelon.
Brood of the tortoise shell lamenting turtle dove.

Psalm

On a scratchy, immortal, late nineteen-forties recording,
Yehudi Menuhin and Isaac Stern
With concentrated vigor so tenderly each

Punctilious chord's excruciations play
In the Bach violin concerto you can almost
Hear the suffering Christ recoil from each

Exacting contraction. The quiver of the gutstrings.
Apollo's bow. On a scratchy vinyl recording,
Yehudi Menuhin and Isaac Stern:

Hebraic harpists striking the Marsyan note.

Ganymede

No matter how many times, or how tenderly,
I lifted my tepid, implacable pet turtle,
His swivel head, and limbs, withdrew inside—

Until he was back in his bleak aquarium.
As if like Arjuna he had finally mastered
Krishna's Second Teaching: *Retract the senses.*

And yet, little gray-cowled monk with wrinkled lids,
Splayed on a painted rock near a tin of water,
When I picked you up by your shell, and held you there,

Suspended in midair, I felt your pulsing fear,
Even through your armor of dull-green plating;
As Zeus once whisked away his Ganymede—

But more like the clutch of those scavengers I saw
On Salisbury Beach, the seagull-harpies,
Whose talons won't let you go, till they're high enough

To let you drop—on rocks that break your shell.
O blessèd creature! Something drew me to you
Instead of the others, there in the pet shop window:

The great horned toad, illustrious chameleon.
Fortified friend, recalcitrant carapace:
Achilles' shield, on which the world was engraved.

Artifact

In the comic fable, "Aeschylus Dead," there's a line
About scholars that's worthy of Aristophanes:
A bald eagle dropped, on his shiny bald head, a turtle.

The Moulourian Rock is sacred to Leucotheia,
But the cove is cursed. Like Agamemnon's bath,
It bubbles with blood. There, Skiron, they say, fed strangers

To giant snapping turtles. But justice was served
When Theseus hurled Skiron into the cauldron.
On the topmost ridge is a carving of Zeus the Thrower,

Preserved in amber. And amber-eyed that "semi-
human" Greek tortoise Peter Levi describes,
Glaring at him from a case in the British Museum.

Snow

When lilacs last in the dooryard bloomed, my father
Came home from work early, the only time
That ever happened. With his butcher's apron still on

He slouched on the sofa, and watched the horse-drawn casket,
And every two minutes got up to fix the picture—
His shot of Metaxa untouched on the TV tray.

But the snow kept falling, as if my father was never
Far from his village, on windy Kyllene's peak,
Where the messenger god is carved from supple juniper.

Now one of the rabbit-ears, topped with a wad of tinfoil,
The one that always kept sinking down to one side,
Is Hermes' wand, escorting more shades through the screen.

Stele

In the famous frieze of Orpheus and Eurydice,
The one at the Naples *Museo Nazionale*
(Though once it was used to mark a young wife's grave),

Each lover, to Rilke, is touching the other so lightly,
Their trembling seems untouched by fear of parting.
Each lover so full, he says, of tenderness,

Possession plays no part in their desire,
Like figures about to merge in a ballroom mirror.
Oblivious love. Music that froze Oblivion.

Orpheus is holding his lyre. Which means that beyond
The frieze the writhing snakes in the Gorgon's hair
Have been put to sleep, or turned themselves to stone.

Orpheus is holding his lyre. A flock of notes
Still hangs in the air—the only birds in Avernus.
Released from his torturous wheel, as it ticks to a halt,

Ixíon thinks his luck has turned at last.
Now Sisyphus straightens up, like Leopardi's
Laborer, about to sing at the end of his day.

Still, here in the *stele,* each pair of stone feet is moving
Its pivoting sandals in another direction,
As Hermes taps Eurydice on the shoulder,

Cutting in on the last dance of the night,
That dance the carving depicts in the Naples museum,
Though once it was used to mark a young wife's grave.

Salt

If "ancient salt," as the poet once said, is still
"The best packing," then my childhood ear
Was steeped in it whenever I got an earache—

Though almost as soon as I felt the pain flare up
So did the match that lit the jets of our stove.
Even now, lying in bed, I still can hear it,

The sizzle of table salt in a shiny skillet
She always called a *tigáni,* and just by recalling
The rhyming Greek word for heating it up, *zestáni.*

Like Morse code for all those tiny particles
Passing back through the semiconductor coils
Of the earliest hearing that I can still remember:

That staticky crackle of salt, when a hot compress
Was being prepared, at the other end of the hall,
And I could pick up the signal of comfort's approach.

Salt like the salt I saw in my father's store,
Preserving the sallow look of the flayed lamb-shanks
That hung, encrusted, from glinting hooks in the freezer.

Salt that was poured into a striped white sock
My mother pried open between her thumb and forefinger—
Then tied a knot in it, like a tourniquet.

Once the firm pressure of an open hand
Was enough to soothe the ache in my eardrum, that throbbing
Membrane I now know is called the tympanum.

The words on my laptop screen are liquid crystal.
The glitter she poured was sand in an hour glass.
The stretchy white sock was meant for the foot of a runner.

Homemade remedy, made from salt of the earth,
Steady my fear by pressing your warmth to my ear.
Muffle the feather-light steps of the messenger god

When he comes, too soon, to lead me down the dark hall.

Trismegistus

Praxiteles carves him perfectly naked—
Without the wingéd sandals and party hat,
Cradling baby Eros in the crook of his elbow.

His messenger's fleeting smile itself the message.
His sinewy body itself the snake-enrapt scepter
That turns him invisible. A healing god.

His shadow the shade that tells you you're a shade.
Even more flawless that anonymous one
I saw in Alexandria: *Irony*

Incarnate engraved on his empty pedestal.

Aubade

Once the upright bow had been bent, Odysseus
Arching it back like a sapling to hook the string,
Homer says he plucked it like a harp—

As if in that majestic commanding gesture
The hero and bard had struck the identical note
And made the tense air hum with implication.

And then, before the arrows began to fly,
The taut string twanged as it sang like a darting swallow
That comes in the thaw of spring, when the grass stands up

Like the hair on the suitors' necks. The Bow and the Lyre,
Our royal instruments, vibrant with homecoming.
The dark ages over forever. The Greek language

Returning from smoldering Troy, centuries later,
A catalogue of ships, with names to come.
Resonant chords, like the chokers of chicken wire

Telemachus would use to "string up the sluts"
Who slept with the groaning suitors. Now louder and higher,
Inspired by the prow and the fire, the singers

Pitch their required songs, as if a wedding
Celebration were taking place inside.
Telemachus making sure the feet of the girls

Were only an inch or two off the marble floor,
Festooned with gore—"to watch them dance their jig,"
The old nurse chortled. As they celebrated the marriage

Of Bow and Lyre, the girls were dancing on air.
Though the suitors' clans would seek revenge tomorrow,
The chariot of Dawn held back its glossy steeds

For the royal couple to consummate their love.

THE SCHOLARS CRITIQUE PAUSANIAS' STYLE

"The problem with his *Guide to Greece* is this:
The place itself does not exist, apart
From its family trees, its myths and monuments.
What happened to the vineyards? That drooping pedant
Goes stalking knowledge as if the ripest grapes,

At least to his glazed eyes, had already withered—
Blasted by acid rain or the Furies' curse.
But should some marble pergola sprout a marble
Thyrsus, his prose turns faintly purple, infused
By tangled, intoxicated accounts of Bacchus.

Thrilled as he is to enter famous Greek cities,
He's oblivious to their inhabitants, as if
Those ancient gates were emptied of all their people;
Then, spellbound by funeral urns, he wonders aloud
Who's coming to the sacrifice, but says it

In tones as level and dry as those silent towns.
If he stops on his way to the summit of Mount Olympus,
And spends the night beneath the sagging thatch roof
Of some bickering, elderly couple, we never hear it—
That low vernacular older than Homer's gods.

All superstition, except in the form of art,
Arouses in him fresh tirades of measured disgust.
But the sacred rites he witnessed at Eleusis
Are still *mysterion:* not to be discussed.
It's hard to know if and when he's being ironic,

His irony's *that* inadvertent, lacking pitch.
Or, he's so possessed by it it's ubiquitous.
He rarely quotes from any historian's work,
But writes his history from memory.
This method no doubt accounts for most of his errors.

Pausanias may declare *it was all one winter*
Between the battle of Gaza, where Ptolemy
Defeated Demetrius, and Salamis,
The battle in which Demetrius defeated
Ptolemy, but in fact there really are six . . ."

Asclepian doctor of the deadpan demeanor,
Now that nothing eases what Cesar Pavese
Once called "the nausea of reoccurrence"—
Nothing except the knowledge that nothing changes
What Fate or our DNA has already written,

Write it again, our Greek generic script,
Whose meds you prescribe in the plainest possible terms:
Study the ruins. All áffect flat as that.
"Dependable dullard . . . Dull beyond description."
Yadda, yadda, yadda as they say in *Elláda.*

IDIOT SAVANT

I found this while searching the sites for Pausanias:
"His Guide is now known only to savants;
Those who, on account of the infinity
Of curious and singular researches
That it contains, have made it their favorite text."

That quote is taken from Father Nicolas Gédoyn,
A French Enlightenment encyclopedist.
Less than a century later, cannonballs strike
The Parthenon's fluted columns. To mark the new
Millennium, those ancient sandstone Buddhas

Blasted to bits. Imagine a one man walking
Wikipedia, on a mountain road
In Arcadia. As famished for vanished arcana
As the Library of Alexandria
Before it was Borges. Everywhere marvels, and all

Recorded with a politely skeptical tone
But nonetheless meticulous detail—
Like someone telling him something, say, about
The Sibyl in a basket. Obsessive-compulsive
Pausanias as the Rain Man. And Noah's Ark.

GORGON

Athena Promachos: offered to Athens after
Marathon. And soon, too soon, the Trophy
Of the Champion was shipped to Rome.
But much, much later, in late Byzantium,
The scribe Nicetas saw her in Constantinople—
Before she was smashed to bits by a drunken mob.
He says the flawless serene of Phidias
Had wrought such frenzy no one could bear the sight
Of even a mere stone image of courage and wisdom.
After the First Crusade, they fancied Athena's
Outstretched hand might summon the host of invaders
Out of the west . . . The lucid absurd of your words,
Nicetas, our Byzantine recording angel,
Incised like a Gorgon breastplate of Lapiths and Centaurs.

ACHILLES IN THE UNDERWORLD

It's when Odysseus sees him in the gloom,
Surrounded by all those handsome young men in their prime,
We hear his awe: "Even here, even way down here,

Son of Peleus, you're still the prince of princes."
"Better to be a live dog than be a dead king,"
Achilles replies, telling the truth about hell.

And that's when Odysseus tells him about the boy,
How he always emerges from the fighting unscathed—
The prowess of Neoptolemus at Troy.

And now Achilles' shade, "ecstatic with joy,"
Will over the meadows dappled with asphodel
Go striding off, as if Elysium

Meant hearing news of his son, the killing machine . . .
But that's when my father's phantom puts down his cleaver
And growls in guttural Greek to Uncle Peter,

Who's feeding hamburger meat to the grinder's teeth:
"Did I work like a dog so my kid might die in the jungle?
If Yorgo gets drafted I'll send him to Ákovos,

And he can stay in the village and help his cousins
Work the damned fields. At least he'll be safe up there . . ."
And then again the three-headed dog will sing

By grinding its teeth, and I'm back in Book Eleven,
Just as the great Achilles goes stalking off
From Odysseus, and makes the asphodels tremble.

FIVE

ON SIR JAMES FRAZER'S NOTE TO THE CATALOGUE OF OLD TREES IN PAUSANIAS

For the oaks at Ilium, shading the tomb of Ilus,
See the generations of leaves still falling,
Mutatis mutandis, in Homer and in Virgil;

As to Olympia's wind-silvered leaves, consult
The victory wreaths in BÜTTICHER'S BAUMKULTUS
(The same that were used when the games were held in Berlin);

For those oleanders winding along Eurotas,
See the oleanders along the winding Alphaeus;
For Athena's Gift, the ungrafted Acropolis olive,

Append Thelpousa, where up from the rocks surged what
They claimed was wild Poseidon's offspring: a fountain
With the blood of a god and a mane of lapus lazuli;

For each elderly pair of entwined ilex, endearingly
Glossed as Baucis and Philemon, Thracian forests
Of cypress and poplar, those bristling evergreen isolates;

As to the slender palm tree on sandy Delos,
The one that was known as Nausikaa, Cicero
Saw it too, and calls it "her" in a letter;

For the fragrance of lemons that turns the Aegean golden,
Consult *The Odes of Kalvos;* for the flicker of light
That fissures the honeyed fig, see *The Orchards of Syon;*

For Dodona's Oak of Zeus, Pausanias notes
That it still spoke, but only when shaken by rock-
Pigeons and wood-doves, and these were never called Sibyls;

For the Syrian laurel that sprouts such fleeting gold hair,
Study Bernini's Daphne, whose writhing trunk
Still freezes the racing god in stunned midstride;

As to the oldest of all, the willow of Samos,
All that's left is The Sanctuary of Hera,
Whose blackened hearth was small as the hearths of the houses;

As to that spreading plane-tree that once sagged under
The weight of groaning partisans, ask your village
Cousins about its shady familial branches;

For the silk of the *stéfana,* those marriage crowns
That Mrs. Tsiótos wove together in Winthrop,
See the crowns of the orange trees in Sellasía;

More lists of old trees can also be found in Pliny
And Theophrastus, but not the Trees of Laertes,
Which even Pausanias could never locate—

Except as those trees the stranger knows by heart,
And by whose fruit a lost, disheveled father
Identifies his son, Odysseus.

STEFANA

One winter morning, a month or so after my cousin
Christina's wedding, which makes me ten, and veils
The trees in snow, I stopped in my tracks before
The open door to the room where Mrs. Tsiótos,
My best friend's mother, wove the *stéfana*.

Hand-woven wedding crowns, so finely made
They were used in ceremonies all over Boston,
And sometimes as far away as Astoria,
New York. And once, by special overnight
Delivery, a pair was sent to Chicago.

The door was open, but there was no one there
At the wooden table that faced some frozen branches
In the gabled windows. The twigs were glazed with ice,
But moving in the breeze, as tree-flickered light
Played over a pair of wire hoops on the table.

Circles of wire without their flowers, but shining
In the winter light as if the aura of spring
Was already glinting there, caught in the coils
That dexterous fingers would weave through orange blossoms
As white as the snow on the crowns of the trees outside.

On the wooden table were spools of colored thread
At various lengths of unraveling, and a pair
Of open scissors with hooks at the finger-holes.
And a little wheel on a stand, wound with ribbon,
Shimmering ribbon to tie the crowns together

Before the young bride and groom stood facing each other
In front of the altar, wearing the snow-white blossoms.
But where was the stuff to make the petals of flowers
Not meant to fade, like the *stéfana* I saw
In a glass-covered box above my parents' bed?

Under the table, in a wicker basket full
Of lacy strips cut up like bits of doilies.
If I had peeked inside the brass keyhole
Of naked revelation, or lifted a fern
And caught the rosy glimmer of the goddess

Rising from her bath in a mountain spring,
I couldn't have felt the shiver of violation
Any more keenly than seeing those *stéfana*
Above my parents' bed. One over the other
Their petals pressed together. But lying there

On the wooden table was shiny wire, the same
Stiff kind of wire that kept my parents' clothes
Dangling from hangers in their dark closets.
(Separate closets with their different smells.)
In the gabled windows the maples were giant crystals

Whose frosted facets refused to melt in the sun.
(By autumn they'd flutter like flames.) Directly behind me,
Stacked up under the shade of an attic stairwell,
About twenty empty, round white boxes were waiting
For Mrs. Tsiótos to finish their *stéfana,*

Narrow boxes lined with crepe, like the ones for ladies'
Felt hats I saw when my mother shopped at Filenes.
Each satin lid was tense as the skin of a drum.
Soon the weddings would be starting in Boston,
New York, or even as far away as Chicago.

> My friend was waiting for me to play with him
> In another room at the other end of the same
> Back hall, that short back hall when I was ten.

RELATIVE

We knew that his name wasn't really *Singeneé*—
But that's what everyone called him: "Relative."
Our uncle who liked to play that trick with a quarter.

First the bright round coin in his open palm,
As plain as day, as if to deny there was any
Hocus Pocus, before he closes his hands.

Next thing his fists move slowly back and forth,
As he mutters something under his breath, in Greek;
Then both held out for one of us to choose.

No coins have yet been placed over anyone's eyes.
My cousins and I are small and easily dazzled.
We get it wrong, but that prolongs the magic.

So *Singeneé* would go through the motions again,
His cobbler's cheek like wrinkled leather, his brassy
Molars as dimly lit as his basement shop,

Where our secondhand shoes are made to shine for first day
Of school. And now one fist and then the other
Unfurled to show us how the money vanished.

But something sang in me each time he feigned
That empty-handed, wide-eyed surprise, knowing
He'd find the quarter tucked behind someone's ear.

Singeneé. Now sing it again in me.
Like one for whom everything under the light of the moon
Is water under the bridge, the moon's dark water.

I coin your name as the term for its passing gleam.
As once, at Soulla's wedding, you gave me change
To toss at the feet of the dancing bride, for luck.

ICONOSTASIS

In a monastery high up in the mountains of Crete,
Not far from a church with a bombed-out roof, I stand
Before an altar that's four-hundred years old,

And wonder how it survived so many invasions.
That's when the monk takes me around the back,
And shows me the jigsaw pattern behind the panels,

Tracing it with his finger while telling me how
The whole thing comes apart, and that each piece
Is small enough to be safely carried away,

As always happens, he says, when there's an invasion.
And as long as the occupation lasts—which could
Mean decades, if not centuries, filled with bloodshed—

Each family's asked to keep one piece of the altar
Hidden away, inside their house, high up
In the mountains of Crete. And once they're finally gone,

Those hordes of infidels and wild crusaders
Who, as the monk is quick to point out, were no more
Barbaric to the Greeks than the Greeks themselves,

The altar is pieced together again. And then,
After all the bloodshed, the people stand before it
And pray to the powers that protected them:

The Virgin's hands, the Dove, the Logos incarnate.
And this is what's known as *iconostasis:* standing
Face to face with the images of God.

It fits together, he says, like a jigsaw puzzle.

ATHANASIOS

As long as the small white bulb in the votive lamp
Still shone when my room got dark, as dark as the night

Outside, it served, for a time, that light, as a night-light.
High up in the corner, where the icons were.

So all night long, as long as the bulb stayed on,
That pair of Byzantine faces, aglow in my room.

One was the Virgin holding her child, the other
Some prophet in red velvet robes, with a furry beard

And my father's name, in Greek, *Athanásios.*
That silver lamp, with its looping tea-kettle handle

And polished gleam, just like the one that steamed
When Aladdin made his wish. (And down from the ceiling

By three brass chains so lightly the lamp still hovers,
Collecting dust—as long as the spiders, as I

Remember, suspend it from longer, gossamer lines.)
High up in my childhood bedroom, above those icons

Whose lamp-lit eyes were never in the dark,
A pale, faintly quivering halo was cast on the ceiling.

If I couldn't sleep, I was told to tell myself stories.
When my father got really sick, and his heart almost stopped,

My mother would pray to *Panagía*—each night,
In my room, when she thought my eyes were closed, I saw her

Looking urgently up at the Virgin Mary
Looking down at her from a dark blue hood.

(Those fervently moving lips, and that wooden icon
Void of expression.) The Christ child was younger than me,

But looked much older. He sat on his mother's lap,
With an open book as big as the Yellow Pages

Cradled upon one arm. When I tried to pronounce
My father's name, in Greek, with his other hand

The Christ child kept two fingers pressed to his lips.
Athanásios, the prophet, was about to speak.

AUSTERITY MEASURES I

Too young to turn a blind eye to his glowering glass one,
But old enough to recoil from that pickle barrel
It always recalled. The oak lid's airtight, implacable
Seal repulsing his prying hands—till hunger
Propped it open, just as a rusty, unruly
Stave sprang up, and cost him half his vision.
Cyclopic Europe. And helpless, free-floating anger.
Pappoúli. Preserved in those briny dark pools of his story.

Not even the man of many turns, as he turns
The sharpened olive spike, can make me wince
Like those pickles that came at the price of darkness visible.
Unglazed, unmoving: an eye for an immigrant's eye
As blue as a cloudy marble. Or the morning sky
Over Athens today, as scavengers work the barrels.

* * *

He left his village at fifteen. Never went back.
Sent money whenever he could. But now, at fifty,
For once he closes his store for more than a week.
But first, for a month, he fasts. And every Sunday
Goes to church. And even receives Communion.
(So as not to *sully Hellás* is how he put it.)
Takes only one suitcase. Big as a crate of melons,
It's velvet inside, with frilly satin pockets.

Forty years on my father returns, as fires
Are closing in on the Parliament building in Athens.
My mother's shade is burning again with indignant,
Astonished, exasperated pride as she opens
My father's suitcase and finds there's nothing in it.
Then their caskets' frilly insides close over their faces.

AUSTERITY MEASURES II

I was reaching for *Lyric Life,* when something else
Flew off the topmost shelf of gilded volumes
By Angelos Sikelianos, and landed,
Without a flutter, face down on the library floor.
A slender pamphlet, by accident dislodged
Along with a little glinting swirl of dust-motes.

Both of the covers were blank, but even before
I saw *The Feast of the Dead* it felt like lifting
The damp, anonymous lid of an ancient jar.
Roughly fifteen pages, stapled together
Between two yellowed pieces of plain brown cardboard.
The ragged edge suggested a box-cutter's razor.

When I showed it to Stratís Haviaras, he called it
"Contraband poetry," and said it was smuggled
Out of the country during the occupation.
Blotches of light-blue ink had bled through the pages,
As if the mimeograph machine might well
Have run off reams of pure Aegean nostalgia—

But the poet of wild, oracular flight had set down
Lines as dry and austere as the penciled inscription:
*Eva Sikelianos, Athens, Nineteen
Forty-two.* The very same Eva Palmer
Who once performed in Doric Modernist chiton
With Isadora Duncan's troupe, at Delphi.

And now the feast of the dead on the evening news,
Crouched inside their crowded agora of cardboard
Houses, and chewing on cardboard sandwiches.
But no telling Stratís how cold and hungry he was
When Panzer tanks patrolled the Parthenon,
And it cost "an arm and a leg for a loaf of bread."

Just contraband poetry, whose lyric life
Is to drop from a library shelf like a frozen bird
From a winter branch. A nightingale so dead
It sets the dust-motes dancing. But not to stir up
Any more stricken ghosts in Grecian costume—
Just Eva, who once performed with Isadora.

SIX

CLEARING MY THROAT

But this time my middle-aged ear was incredulous:
Those choked-off, roiling, inchoate clots of phlegm
That kept getting stuck halfway: they sounded exactly
Like my father, who never got past sixty.
I heard him in the phlegm, my father's phantom—

Breathless, yet still trying to cough it up.
Struggling hard to tell me something, in Greek.
But since the bloodless shades are helpless to speak,
The best he could do was to make it gurgle up
In my throat, from the muck and mucus of Tartarus.

OLYMPIAN 14

—Pindar

Always close to the current that flows to us
From Kaphisos, and never far from the grass
The beautiful horses graze on, royal sisters,
Who love the open fields so much you make
Orkhomenos your home, and by whose grace
It's over time that only the blackest furrows
Are turned into richest loam, like perfect strophes:
Hear my song that springs from praise of you.

Guardians of the Minyai's ancient race,
Everything in the world we mortals admire,
And sing about, is nothing without your blessing.
If someone's a brilliant speaker, or lovely to look at,
Your radiance is what makes their excellence
The center of our attention. Without the Graces,
Even the gods in heaven would be without
Their festivals and stately circle dances.
There are triple thrones on Mount Olympus, and there
The Holy Graces are sitting beside Apollo,
Who holds the golden bow—up there in the clouds
Forever flowing with Father Zeus in his glory.

Highest of the daughters of Heaven's King:
Just as a glance from gleaming Aglaia's eyes
Or Euphrosuna's smile is always enough
To ensure success, just so may your delight
Accompany our delight in these choral odes
Performed for the sake of heaven. And Thalia, you,
Turn to these dancers whose appreciation
For our good fortune is still expressed in steps
So light the earth beneath their feet appears
To flower with the fluent joy that's always
Thanks to Thalia. If I can keep my lines
Turning as gracefully as these lines of dancers

Are turning, you'll know I've come to celebrate
Asopikos, offspring of the Minyai,
With songs of triumph measured the Lydian way.

Echo, go now, down to the dark-walled house
Down where Persephone lives, and find Kleodamos,
And tell him that someone he knows was crowned today
With olive leaves, at the foothills of Olympia:
A boy whose hair the breeze will never turn silver,
Now that we know that the name Asopikos
So brightly evokes the flutter of Victory's wings.

Echo, go now. Deliver the news to his father.

AGGANIS

The Kleft is bleeding. The mountain springs are gushing.
—Modern Greek Folksong

I.

The biggest icon in our parish church
Was the one in the basement, over the water bubbler
Across from the sallow floor of the basketball court.
A life-size portrait of Harry Agganis, "The Golden
Greek," in his Boston Red Sox uniform.
By the trophy case. With its tribal memorabilia.

When I'd bow my head for a drink, my eyes were level
With scuffed black cleats still guarding the first-base line.
Both up on his toes and at ease. In crimson greaves.
His leather mitt was small as his open hand.
His sculpted jaw was shadowed by his visor.
Sunday school was over whenever I stood there,

Reciting his legacy like a liturgy:
At twenty-one, the number one pick of the Cleveland
Browns, and quarterback heir to the great Otto Graham.
At twenty-three, the clean-up hitter behind
Immortal Ted Williams. At twenty-six he was dead.
Struck down by a fast-moving tumor that lodged in his thigh—

Thrombos, my father called it. Coagulant clot.
Dithyrambic beat. Line shot to the heart. *Thrombos.*
My mother could feel me kick when she sat on a bench
In the Lynn Commons, across the street from the church.
My mother, superstitious, and fearing another
Miscarriage, refused to enter "Harry's wake."

Umbilical, overanxious, inchoate *agon.*
The stream of mourners, most of them laborers.
Engulfing sorrow, already in embryo.

The wooden bench in the shade of Doric oaks.
The blood in the womb as warm as that day in June.
Agganis-Adonis, gored by the wild boar's tusk.

II.

Under the dying hero's portrait, I bowed
My head to the little bubbling jet. Ice-cold
As a village spring from Logganiko, the water
Gushed lugubrious against my tongue.
If I thought about the bursting blood clot, the bubbler
Left the taste of rusty pipes in my mouth.

Inside their long glass case, the polished trophies
All had his name on them. Their fluent, definitive
Pivots still welded by heel and toe to their marble
Pedestals—forever alloyed to their poise,
And the crouching boys who shadowed them, transfixed.
The Golden Greek, like a goldfish in glory's dark

Aquarium. When I pressed my face to the glass,
It was cool and smooth as the shining brow of Agganis,
Lying in the open, flowered bier of the martyr.
Embalmed in a snapshot. His death announced by the *Boston
Herald*'s yellowed clippings . . . How long for a poem's
Unforced gestation? How far from Lynn was Sparta?

What leaf-fringed village legend from Logganiko
Haunted that silver untarnished olive wreath
Propped on a plaque at the center of the trophy case:
A gift from Frederica, Queen of Greece.
Its spiky metal branches a halo of thorns
Too prickly for our bloodless Byzantine Christ,

Still floating up from the Cross like a butterfly
About to slough the silk of its torn cocoon,

As the psalters droned and it all went over our heads
In late November of nineteen sixty-three.
But the gift from Frederica was stark as the fricative
Consonants that made me recoil from her name.

Aeons before I heard of Pindar or Horace,
Even the great Achilles was somewhere down there,
In our church basement, crowned by the Queen of Orkus.

PAUSANIAS AT THE TOMB OF HYACINTH

In Amyklai, and still standing above
The sepulcher, there's a statue of Apollo
So stiffly fashioned in the archaic way
That if not for the bronze sheen of his face and hands
You might mistake him for a marble pillar,
Forever frozen there above the tomb.

The altar is engraved with various gods
Escorting a naked Hyakinthos to heaven,
Led by the awful Fates. I was surprised
To see dark bristles incised on his flawless cheek.
And then there's the legend of the crimson flower.
Nikias' image of him is more refined.

Augustus brought it back from Alexandria,
And when he died, Tiberius kept the painting
On permanent display, in the emperor's temple.
And it's still there, in Rome, and that's where I saw it,
The famous Hyakinthos of Nikias.
And everywhere in Arcadia now I hear

Of Hadrian's Antinous, already proclaimed
The newest god. I never met him, except
As the boy reflected in pools of Roman villas.
Narcissus of the Nile they call him, in Egypt,
Where Hadrian lost him forever, and founded *Anti-
noupolis,* the city he built in the desert.

And even way up here, in the mountains surrounding
Mantineia, the fierce Lakonians
Strike coins that cast him as *Antinous Pan.*

ON THE DECK OF A SHIP

—Cavafy

It's *him*, this little drawing done in pencil—
At least as far as its faint gray outline goes.

Just a quick sketch. I made it on the deck
Of a moving ship, in the middle of the day,

That shimmering day on the blue Ionian Sea.
It looks a lot like him. But just the same,

It's not the face I draw from memory now.
His mood at any moment might turn dark,

Back when the waves of noon were all around us.
He was more beautiful than my sketch of him.

And there, in my mind's eye, I picture him
Without a trace of time, the time gone by.

All of these things took place in the distant past:
The pencil sketch, the ship, and the afternoon.

ARGONAUTS

—Seferis

My companions. I could always count on them
To get the job done. They never once complained

Of the biting frost or the parching thirst. Even as
Their backs were being lashed by wind and rain

They were steady as oaks, in stroke after even stroke—
Themselves the driving force that stays the course

When the treacherous currents shift. That crew was a good one.
They drew back their oars without ever lifting their eyes,

Breathing in rhythm, sunup to sundown, their sweating
Faces as sanguine as the day was long.

Approaching that desert island that lay to the west,
By the Cape of Barking Dogs, the island famous

For its Arabian figs, all of them suddenly
Broke into song, without ever losing sight

Of the task at hand: *if the soul is to know itself*
It must look into the soul of someone else,

Or so they sang as their dipping blades struck gold
As they struck the water's mirror, and shattered twilight.

Nearing one island another was on the horizon.
One sea flowed into the next one, and who could say

If those shrill strange cries were only gulls and seals
Or the wild laments of mothers mourning their children?

While other seekers were lost in search of the Great
Alexander's tomb, obsessed with treasures buried

Somewhere in Asia, we anchored in narrow inlets,
Engulfed by evening's musk. All night the night birds

Sang in the dark, and the water we cupped in our hands
Was the joy, sheer joy, we harbored in memory.

But nearing one island another was on the horizon.
And I over time couldn't tell the rising and falling

Blades of their oars apart from the rowers themselves,
Could not distinguish between the cut of the prow,

The rudder's wake, and my shipmates in the craft.
If the soul is to know itself it has to shatter

Itself in the water's mirror, or so they sang
As one by one my companions closed their eyes

And the rowing benches emptied. Then each man's oar
Was planted upon the shoreline where he sleeps.

And there is no one now who knows their names.

THE ROWERS

Oblivious to everything but the beat of their oarlocks,
Over and over they strike the dark night water's surface
Into swirls the quicksilver craft instinctively recoils from.

The irresistible singers stand on a reef of bones.
The rowers never look up. The doldrums are all around them.
Across the Sirens' mouths flows nightfall's streaming hair.

In the brightness bleached from their marrow the heaps of bones cry out
To the writhing hero, whose wrists are cut by rawhide cords.
The swaying mast is pointing to stars that sail above it.

Beyond the midnight pull of the moon, the rowers bend
Their rounded backs to their wooden blades. To them the currents
Calling them home are dim as a kitchen's fluorescent hum.

The honey of Hymettos has stopped their ears with wax.

LAMENT FOR THE MAKERS

Arion of Methymna, in Myron's sculpture,
Rides on a dolphin. Translucent as the waves,
Whose cresting bronze the dolphin's arching torso
Is plunging through, Arion's robes are drenched
In what clings to his skin. The singer's mouth is open.
Everything flows. They leap for joy, in tandem.

But there's another splash in the sculpture, and that's
Thamyris the Thracian's lyre, his instrument drowning
In Homer's Dorian River. But some Messenians
Claim that he flung his lyre into the River
Balyra. As if by sounding βαλλω and λυρα
Balyra means what they say. He threw it away.

Did it strike too close to Homer for him to sing
About what the jealous Muses did to his teacher,
As the myths make all too clear: *they gouged out his eyes.*
Blindness never darkened Homer's vision
Of rosy-fingered Dawn, but once Thamyris
Saw bright Earth go blank, his song was eclipsed.

(Unless the famous line about rosy Dawn
Is quoting poor Thamyris, his vision restored
Each time we read the line and see dark earth
Turn bright again as Homer sings the refrain,
Recalling the pain, of his disillusioned teacher.)
Trained in the healing ways of Asclepius,

Pausanias refused to blame the Muses
For blinding the bard. It must be, he felt, some rare,
Ocular disease, opaque as the oracles.
Or maybe the gift of poetry itself
Was a form of pathology. As in the famous
Painting by Polygnotos: *The Doomed Singers.*

And there, Thamyris' hair has all fallen out.
His lyre lies at his feet. The gutstrings have snapped.
His arms just hang there. His gouged-out eyes are gouache.
Apollo is cast in the shadow of brilliant Marsyas,
Who teaches Olympos to play the double flute
As a Phrygian waits, with a laurel wreath and a knife.

Leaning against Persephone's willow, Orpheus
Grips his harp in one hand, and sweeps his other
Across the vines, as if they were unplucked chords.
He doesn't appear as a priest, in somber gray mantle
And fox-skin cap, as the vulgar Thracians have him,
Nor as the Romans do, with a golden tiara

And purple cummerbund. To the Greek on the other
Side of Persephone's willow, Orpheus still
Appears as a Greek. Both men in Doric chitons,
Promedon not a musician. And yet his cocked
Ear is key to the composition. Promedon:
Record collector supreme of Orphic song.

Wedged into the painting's lower left-hand corner,
Sakadas is no bigger than a cicada.
His skin is shiny and hard as a pinewood plectrum.
His scales are all aglitter. Like all the other
Shrill cicadas, his pitch was perfect, once.
Sakadas: his tiny, steadfast, insect face

Still clenched like a fist. *As if the poet was trying
To scream with all his might,* is how Seferis
Described the skull of Kalvos, after seeing
The photographs of its corpse, exhumed in England.
Andreas Kalvos, who lost his island voice
For fifty years, but whose writer's block still spoke

To Seferis' fear, as if he was reading an x-ray
Of lock-jawed silence as he looked down, in silence,
At the black and white image of Kalvos, decomposed.
His wizened skull, in the snapshot, a shrunken melon.
His only book an ode to his sunlit island.
Our Derek Walcott forever on the horizon.

Unearth, from Lincolnshire, the poet's broken lyre,
And back to Zakynthos convey the bones of Kalvos.

Arion of Methymna, in Myron's sculpture,
Rides on a dolphin. Translucent as the waves,
Whose cresting bronze the dolphin's arching torso
Is plunging through, Arion's robes are drenched
In what clings to his skin. The singer's mouth is open.
Everything flows. They leap for joy, in tandem.

SEVEN

TIBULLUS IN SPARTA

Out of obdurate earth, sown with the Dragon's teeth,
And fields where the flocks of fattened *próbata*
Are kept in line with a growl and a well-aimed stone,
My great-uncle Paul: still famous among the sheepfolds
For both his wooden flute and his mild demeanor.

Golden scales for the silver fleece of each numbered,
Ruminant head, uplifted by music too soft
For the village brutes—ankle-deep in the shambles.
For him, even the calves would climb the cliffs.
Out of killing cousins and crossing streams still called

By their *Turkokratía* names, our sweet Tibullus.
His the unwavering, soothing, persuasive voice
Still calling out from the docks to the panicked girl
Who clung to the rail of a ship as it left Piraeus,
In nineteen ten. I saw him whenever young Paul,

His smiling, courteous grandson, would happen to enter
A family function. Then, from across the hall,
Always my heavy-set grandmother, *Aglaía*,
Out of a stuporous haze, would pull herself up
On her chrome walker, and start to amble his way.

SOMEWHERE OUTSIDE MOSUL

The sun is beating down on the jagged outcrop.
About fifty prisoners enter the cul-de-sac
Of a low ravine. The shooters are standing on top.

All but their eyes are masked in tribal scarfs.
The captured Shiites are a shambling lot.
Young, they are wearing t-shirts, sneakers, and blue jeans.

One turns around and looks right into the camera,
But doesn't throw up his hands like that guy in Goya.
Not yet. Before they can switch to another shot,

My mother's long-dead father screams a god-awful
Scream as he wakes from his nap on our parlor sofa.
I'm down on the rug, playing with toys when it happens.

He gives me that look, as if he was back in the Balkans.
I can't know that yet. But *somewhere outside Mosul,*
Panning those echoing, steeped-in-vendetta, cliffs

The voice-over now is Homer's, in village Greek.

EASTER IN THE OVEN

—Kiki Dimoula

The goat was bleating so much its voice had grown hoarse.
Furious, I opened the oven door:
"Knock it off. Our company can hear you."
"But it isn't even lukewarm in here," said the sheepish
Voice from the oven. "And if you don't act quick
Your feast will end in a fast. And what will become
Of your butchery if you ruin the holiday?"

I reached my hand inside. The goat was right
About the oven. Everything I felt—
The forehead, the shins, the neck, the grass, the crags
Of the cliffs—was steeped in slaughter, and frozen solid.

HELLMOUTH

"Go back inside and check on the stove, Yorgo."
Always those same last-minute admonitions

That drove you out of the idling, black Desoto;
Faint palpitation of fear that keeps their voices

Palpably urgent, alive, in their tenseness to hear
If the little red arrows on all the silver knobs

Were pointed straight up, to OFF. And even then,
There was always his *alýtheia?—are you sure?*

And then her more dubious, inquisitive stare.
But had I double checked by touching my hand

To all four stove-rings? I nodded my head, but felt
My culpable fingers singed by copper coils.

And only then it was on to where we were going,
Which almost always meant some relative's house,

Although for them the word was *spíti.* Then always
The sound of *house,* in their tongue, turned over on yours,

As you repeated the sibilant pitch of *spíti.*
So you still go back inside to check on the stove,

Back to those days when smoke unfurled from the oven
Before the door was opened; then Sunday's lamb

In its sizzling pan was lifted with padded mitts,
And set on the counter—which helps you to savor it more,

Till the memory cools. Though not before you catch
A home-cooked whiff of Hellmouth yawning open,

Which History taught them could happen, at any time.
Hellmouth as black as that abandoned hearth

Whose iron kettle still hangs from its hook; as black
As that black Desoto that took you from house to house.

Hellmouth as steeply arched as their mountain church
In Ákovos, the one you enter via

Leviathan's gaping jaws, its livid ceiling
Swarming with murals of demons. It's what was there

In the kitchen, inside that white-hot door left open
For you to see what smoldered inside their fear:

Those village snapshots of emptied houses, whose silence
You enter more deeply now, now that their sockets

Of charred stucco are staring back at you,
As if to say: *No one has seen a thing,*

Not even the witnesses. Which is to say:
"Go back inside and check on the stove, Yorgo."

MYCENAE: PAUSANAIS CONDUCTS A GUIDED TOUR OF THE BURIAL CHAMBERS

Mycenae's stupendous wealth was kept in these vaults,
But its source of water lies outside its limits:
Conducted through subterranean earthenware pipes
And pulsing up from a small perennial spring
The water's purity makes itself clear to the city,
Its hidden freshet a blessing in times of siege.

Agamemnon's here, in this mossy sepulcher,
Beside Eurymedon, his charioteer,
Who stood outside while the king went in for his bath.
There's Atreus, son of that Pelops whose bones the gods
Regurgitated—having swallowed the stew
Concocted by his father, Tantalus.

And there, still snug in their wooden cradle, the twins
Teledamos and Pelops, Cassandra's babies,
Slaughtered with their mother, by Aegisthus
And Clytemnestra. (Outcast Cassandra's remains,
So the Spartans claim, are buried with them, in dark
Lakonian loam obscure as her oracles.)

Elektra, too, in the gloom, she whom her brother
Orestes, after he had murdered their mother,
Offered in marriage to his comrade in arms.
Hellanikos records they had two sons,
Strophios and Medon. These children sleep
Beside their parents, Pylades and Elektra.

Aegisthus and his sadistic paramour lie
Together as well, but well outside the walls.
May the oozing over them serpentine slime of the mud
Forever keep their polluted corpses entwined
In its orgiastic grip, expelled from our city—
And stop their thirsty shades from drinking more blood . . .

That resonant chant is carved in porous sandstone.
How then, you might ask, did these apotropaic walls
Remain so impenetrable? It's *breccia:*
A mix of mortar and horsehair, whose bristling matrix,
Embedded with glassy shards, still glints—*sweet light*—
Whenever prevailing winds pick up from Aulis.

We're passing back through the famous Lion Gate.
Like the tufted ring-walls of Tiryns, the massive scale
And sculpted beasts recall the hand of Kyklops—
I mean the master builder, not the monster.
But none of these giant, twenty-by-thirty foot blocks
As heavy as the ox on the watchman's tongue.

ARLINGTON NATIONAL CEMETERY

Ó-po-po whispered my Arcadian father
As the four of us came over the dazzling slope
Of freshly mown grass aglitter with morning dew.

Open-mouthed, dactylic stress that keeps
The breathless canopy of trees idyllic,
Exactly like in Poussin's painting, where shepherds

Puzzle over an ancient tomb inscribed
Et in Arcadia ego, not knowing what
On earth it means in their neoclassical Eden.

My staggered father knew, yet didn't know,
From World War II, that there could be so many—
So many snow-white crosses, and all of them staked

In appalling, perfectly symmetrical rows.
Ó-po-po he whispered, just softly enough
For us to hear, but not to wake up the rest.

Then further down, beyond the Flame Eternal,
My mother exclaimed, "Oh look—the poor brother!"
And pointed her finger directly at Aeschylus,

Whose words were engraved on the shrine for RFK.
"Look, that's Greek." But it was all in English:
Even in our sleep, that pain which cannot

Forget falls drop by drop upon the heart,
Until, in our despair, against our will,
Comes wisdom through the awful grace of God . . .

Even in bloodless sleep and drop by drop
The lawn aglitter with morning dew a chorus
Sings from deep in the sacred grove of the Furies.

And *look, oh look* and *ó-po-po* I hear it.

OMENS

If one of us happened to drop a spoon while she
Took care of us, she took it for a sign

That company was coming, and sometimes it happened
That almost as soon as the dishes were put away

More dishes were being taken out again—
At least that's how the dull faint chime of a spoon

Still rings a bell, and opens the door for my dead
To keep me company, in memory.

But if it was a fork that happened to fall,
There's no precise expression, even in Greek,

For the evil that might transpire, other than her
Och—och—och, a sound as ominous

And acutely pronged as the fork still lying there
On the kitchen floor as if it waited for you

To pick up the glinting tines you heard in her tone—
Which never fade, unlike the linoleum.

And sometimes she'd ask if our ears were "ringing inside."
Before we could answer she'd summon us to her chair,

And one by one we'd bow our unschooled heads
So she could snap her fingers in front of our ears—

To keep us from hearing whatever was going to happen
Before it happened. Or so she said. And to keep

What she said from going in one ear and out
The other, that crisp, implacable snap of her fingers.

She sat in a high-backed chair. We stood at attention.
She'd come to America when she was thirteen,

From a tiny village near Mount Taíygetós.
She was deathly afraid of thunderclaps and lightning,

And both of her older brothers had taken part
In the secret plot to take back Constantinople.

SAILING TO BYZANTIUM

That shade who woke me up last night was some doom
And gloom great-uncle. His name was Panayóti.
He'd fought at Smyrna, and challenged me on Yeats:

"No golden smithies were there to break the flood
When the altars of Hagia Sophia were streaming blood,
And the golden parrot that clings to its golden palm

Is scared shitless to sing to the Emperor's face
Of what's to come. John Páleológos knows
From those heads across the moat, impaled in rows.

Through flames that cannot singe the poet's sleeve
A falcon goes with a note in its frantic beak:
The City fell on Tuesday." And then he goes back

To Smyrna, and what it was like in 1919—
When the superpowers "conspired to not intervene."
And then he goes back to Yeats, still harping on

That dolphin-torn, that gong-tormented sea.

MINERVA TRITONIA

Horizon-high on her roofless Acropolis.
Brilliance in the brilliance. Born from the gaping-open
Of the sky-god's forehead. And then it dawns on us.
Her level visor impervious to revision.
The Gorgon her shield. But in leafy Alalcomene,
Pausanias saw The Temple to the Abandoned
Child. Athena before she was full-blown Athens . . .
Wisdom unknown, but never, in the woods, alone,
Not yet the stone, implacably smooth blank visage
Above the spear, but here the evergreen stare
Of a little girl lost in the aboriginal dark:
Pallid Athena, owl-eyed with terror.

Uncanny the shrine, and *Triton*'s the name still glossing
The stream that guards it, the murmuring stream that sang
A lullaby once, in leafy Alalcomene.
Sir James Frazer was there, and notes what he saw:
The stones of this overgrown temple have been pried loose,
And are still being torn apart and tossed aside
By a giant ivy tree's tentacular grip . . .
Olive the groves of amorphous buffetings.
Virgin the moss where infant wisdom's oldest
Vestige clings. Totemic the child the emperor
Sulla abducted. Roman the fountain at whose
Fetishistic foot he stood his wooden Tritonia.

Then Sulla assaulted Athens. Erecting his siege
Engines from trees. Dodona's primordial oaks.
Lopped off and lugged from a hundred miles away.
As if the palladium-plundering Greeks had not
Invented the art . . . But how to explain what happened
At Phaiakia, the only city in Homer
That never knew war, and so advanced it might be
Atlantis? Weird, diabolical even, the way
Athena ran to the wandering hero, washed up
On that pristine shore like radioactive waste.

The goddess disguised as a green-eyed girl with a jug
Of sloshing water, calling out *Papou! Papou!*

My children. The first words out of Oedipus' mouth—
The suppliants sprawled at his doorstep's darkening portals,
His blood the blind source of the city's black pollution.
And the plague took Pericles, too. After the brilliant
Oration, bonfires of corpses. The best one could do,
Thucydides wrote, was care for one's neighbor then die.
It starts with a burning forehead, and reddening eyes...
Then bleeding at both ends . . . vomiting and bile . . .
The lightest linen a shirt of fire . . . Athens,
The fervid tongues of its citizens black with contagion.
Some tore off their chitons and plunged in the water tanks,
Or severed their cocks to stop the priapic swelling.

Tangara has a Triton-thing in a jar.
His head is sleek as a frog's in stagnant water.
His human nose and ears have slits for gills.
His greenish-gray eyes recall Minerva's eyes.
His lower half is all one tail, as scaly
As an iguana, and bristling with barnacles.
Damostratos has dissected a piece
Of its petrified scales. Subjected to fire, he writes,
It leaves an odor worse than rotting fish.
Sulla, the savage, died of a strange disease.
Maggots seethed from his skin. A stream of blood
Poured out of his mouth, and from his arching penis.

EIGHT

ORIGINS

Behind the words there is a poem
Behind the poem there is a voice
Behind the voice there is a breath
Behind the breath there must be silence
Behind the silence is where the voice
That speaks the poem is coming from

Inside the thirst there is a well
Inside the well there is no light
Inside the dark there is an echo
Inside the echo there must be longing
Inside the longing is where the water
No bucket can hold is coming from

GRACKLE

Tense as the string my older cousin held taut,
I crouched behind an oak, transfixed by a milk crate
Propped by a stick, and weighted down with a brick.

And a trail of bread set out on the backyard grass.
Bread our immigrant elders said was a sin
To leave on your plate, and even if it was hard

And stale was never ever thrown away.
Before I knew what a grackle was I saw one
Bow his hesitant head to the mouth of our trap.

The sun was almost down. Heraldic he was,
In his glossy, pitch-black, shining plumage. *Awful*—
Godawful—the grackle's cry at the tug of a string.

Helpless our terrified captive, thrashing so wildly
That feathery wisps came floating through the grates.
Triumphant my cousin planting one foot on the crate.

But then he tilts it back. And never again
The up-whoosh of wings so close to my startled ear.
And now there's no escaping that pitch-black bird

Alighting on the grass, in the afterglow
Of *give us this day our daily bread*—as if
He'd come to announce another century

Of steerage, and starving villages, and awful cries.

PALIMPSEST*

You gave me hyacinths first a year ago
That little sanguine flower inscribed with woe
Antinous, Hadrian said, is all I know

And voices singing out of the empty cisterns
Exempt from the vicissitudes of the seasons
A city where nothing exists, not even its ruins

Jerusalem, Athens, Alexandria   Unreal
In the Vale of Glamorgan John Barleycorn burns in a wheel
On the Temple of Zeus, twenty-one Roman shields

A crowd flowed over London Bridge, so many
Here lies Dionysios dead, son of Semele
A lullaby once, in leafy Alalcomene

Sweet Thames, run softly, till I end my song
As a triple knot ties the Lapland wind by its tongue
Selemnus, love's sweet-bitter stream, is endless, then gone

A current under sea picked his bones in whispers
In a shallop made of papyrus she searched for Osiris
Saying more—or less—than this profanes Eleusis

Madame Sosostris, famous clairvoyante
Unmanned he bleeds, as Attis, over the violets
To cover all of Greece I can't dwell on it

Or in memories draped by the beneficent spider
The soul is away, they *shsh,* don't wake the sleeper
The myths are absurd—but now I'm a child, a writer

And crawled head downwards down a blackened wall
With tiny white linens for the mice-gods of Bali
Then flung his lyre into the River Balyra

In which sad light a carvèd dolphin swam
Mistletoe—the golden bough—the thunder besom
In times like these no god in human form

Bestows one final patronising kiss
Each corpse with its clothes left unbuttoned on Karpathos
Praxiteles' *Eros as the cost of Eros*

When I count there are only you and I together
Round the mystic kalends a thousand quaint rituals cluster
If memory serves oblivion's jet-black water

Revive for a moment a broken Coriolanus
Or the rain-king whose guts are ripped out if the sky stays cloudless
In Epidaurus some dream is the viper that cures us

* The first line in each stanza is taken from Eliot's *The Waste Land,* the second is from Frazer's *The Golden Bough,* and the third is from my version of Pausanias' *Guide.* Sir James Frazer's magisterial commentary on Pausanias came out in 1898. Frazer then went on to write *The Golden Bough,* which became a seminal source for *The Waste Land.*

ANDIDORO

Every Easter, and just at the start of Lent,
One of those blue-striped envelopes would be sent
From Greece, containing what it could barely seal:
A rigid cube of bread, wrapped in tinfoil.

Andídoro, the gift in return for a gift.
It was sent by nuns who lived on the edge of a cliff
Above my father's village. Before I could read,
Their stucco house was there, in the pockmarked bread.

Though it didn't have a door, or any windows,
Its roof was an orange crust. *Andídoro.*
Communion bread that never went stale, as long
As I could taste it fresh, in another tongue.

A word that meant more names would go on the list,
The one my mother wrote up when it was Lent,
And sent to the nuns, along with some dollar bills.
Names of our dead, chanted over distant candles.

Andídoro. A lump in the envelope's throat.
Bread baked in an ashen hearth, or so I was told
By the tinfoil's crinkly glow. Ancestral crumb.
Strange valleys where the dark vowels were coming from.

And then, at midnight, on Holy Saturday,
When all the murmuring stopped so suddenly,
Everyone would stand, as our church went dark.
Waiting, with unlit candles, for singing to start.

RECIPROCITY

1

As abruptly as it begins, with a look at blindness
And power, when Athens lost whatever control
Of the sea it had left (and never regained again,
Except for Onassis), the *Guide to Greece* breaks off,
With an image of artistic vision restored,

And a ruined temple surrounded by the sea.
Pausanias got the story from the poet
Anyte, who had it engraved on those marble tablets
Displayed at Epidaurus: *The Words of the Cured*,
Attesting to the skill of the Serpent God.

So too the tinkling of countless tin ex-votos.
Asclepian wind-chimes, shaped like parts of the body.
All kinds of affliction, twisting in the slightest wind.

2

When the painter Phalysios was going blind,
Anyte claims she dreamed of Asclepius,
Who put in her hands a scroll with a waxen seal,
Impressing upon her to give it to the sick man.
A scroll whose seal was real when she opened her dream-stuck,

Tear-filled eyes. And now to Nafpaktos
Anyte sailed, and finding her friend, she put
The thing in his puzzled hands: some rolled-up parchment
He knew would be blank, but opened it anyway.
Opened his opaque eyes, and found his workshop

Radiant, but the world as scumbled as ever.
Mortal vision. Divine revision. He read
What the god demanded of him: *two thousand gold coins.*

3

Epiphanies fade. Anti-epiphanies fade.
More bills to be paid at the local *pharmakío.*
Choose your poison-cure. Athens chose
The sea. On the promontory at Nafpaktos
The temple of healing lying in pieces. The one

Phalysios paid for. So what's it all add up to,
Pausanias: Art gives pleasure but pain is real?
Power is always in flux? As if that vacant
Site on the cliffs, and the sea's encroaching currents,
Were a shrine to seeing. And a form of measure. Anyte's

Lines are addressed to love: *O bronze Kypris,*
Beacon to sailors: ensconced on the sunlit ledge
Your shimmering image is steeped in tremulous waves.

CRICKET SONG

Titivízei. Those twittering cries the blackbird
Makes when it descends to drink from a pure
Mountain spring in late Seferis, a word
That seemed to draw on demotic roots so obscure
I couldn't find it in any of my dictionaries—

Nothing from Oxford's Modern and Byzantine Greek,
Or Liddell and Scott. Then I looked it up in your eyes,
Incredulous as you turned from the kitchen sink
To enlighten my ignorance with a terse couplet
Fresh from your girlhood, a song about what the crickets

Sing at the height of summer. The dripping faucet
Gleams, like a source that goes back to those early poets
Who loved to sing so much they forgot to eat,
So the gods turned the poets into creatures so tiny
That now they feed on the dew. *Titivízei.*

FRANKLIN PARK ZOO

1

Esý, poitís? The phrase still buzzes my ear
It's sibilant, pustulant, sting intact. As if
I'd upset the teeming hive. I'm a petulant, edgy
Nineteen, furious at my parents, blue-collar
Greeks who stressed education but knew nothing
At all about colleges. Or why on earth

I wanted to be a poet. Four years from now
My father will drop dead. But here he's pouring
Brandy for Uncle Panos, who knows a lot
About stocks and bonds, and gives us tips that will keep
My mother secure for the rest of her life. It's Sunday.
The shot of *Seven Star Metaxa* is golden.

2

"You, a Poet? Bah!" The sonorous, basso,
Falstaffian voice from the parlor shadows belongs
To Panos Sakelláris, a hot dog vendor
With a head like Socrates'. As a shepherd boy
He'd learned the songs of love and dispossession,
And sang them in our parlor. When he closed his eyes

We were rolling ours. Then we drank the Turkish coffee
Down to the acrid mud of a tiny stone village
As white as a demitasse cup. Although my uncle
Had never heard of Keats, he helped me to see
The little town on the urn, emptied of its folk.
And showed me his reader's card to the Athenaeum.

3

For decades Tasía and Panos would stand till dusk
At their wooden stall by the zoo in Franklin Park—

A dangerous place after dark. "But the *beasts* are worse
In *Greece,*" my uncle declared, forcing the rhyme,
Which is how I hear him now, still holding court
At our claw-foot mahogany table. "*Moréklavé,*

How dare you speak like that to your parents? Aren't you
Ashamed—*den drépesai?* What college can give you
More than they did, your mother and father, who gave you
Our *glóssa,* and English too? And you would call
Yourself a poet. *Ante sto diávolo . . .*"
And now he shoots me the outstretched, five-fingered curse—

4

And there we are, under the wide Catalpa
Trees in Franklin Park. The zoo's already
Getting dark, though not as dark as our empty
Parlor's shadows will be, on later Sundays.
My father, in feathered fedora, walks ahead.
He carries the baby the same way he does a lamb-shank,

Cradled in his arms—but the baby's squirming around.
My mother's holding me by my five-year-old hand.
Her bright print dress has rhomboid and triangle shapes.
Her hair's a beehive. In the photograph from the zoo
At Franklin Park, we're eating hot dogs that aunt
Tasía has lavished with mustard and relish and ketchup.

Under the shadows of the wide Catalpas
The beasts are behind us, dozing in their cages.

PEREGRINATIONS OF PAUSANIAS

Without Pausanias, Sir James Frazer concludes,
The ruins of Greece would be a labyrinth
Without a clue, a riddle without an answer.
Pausanias says the labyrinth exists—
He saw it, in Crete, at the palace of King Minos,
But wouldn't elaborate upon the twisted
Choreography of its serpentine layout;
And says the stream still flows where Oedipus stopped
On his way to the oracle, before he knew

The blood he washed from his outstretched hands was his father's blood.

> *

Periegesis Hellados wasn't his title,
Nor does Pausanias ever use the phrase.
Ten parchment volumes, one for each mainland province:
Attica, the Argolid, Corinth, Lakonia, Messenia,
Eleia, Achaia, Arkadia, Boetoea, Phokis.
Four centuries later it was Stephanos, scribe
Of early Byzantium, who named the collection.
Stephanos copied the only extant scrolls:
The text that was written, he says, in the author's hand.

The hand that never chose the title, *Guide to Greece.*

> *

Because so many of the actual sites
No longer exist (and even by his own time
Were already nothing but ruins, curios
For Roman tourists), all attempts to map
The polytropic routes Pausanias took
Are sketchy at best, although his dogged approach
To wherever it is he went is always the same:
Walking from the periphery to the *polis,*

Then back to the outskirts again. Over and over,
And every time from a slightly different angle,
Until each approach is also a form of reproach,
And the *topos* he traverses is circumscribed
By steps that can't be traced, except to a place
Where place is voice, and voice is measured in feet.

The steps of advance and retreat. Nation as peregrination.

*

Was it in *Vertigo* or *The Rings of Saturn*
Where Sebald knows a nervous breakdown is coming
But can't stop pacing around and around a windswept
Highland field once soaked in Saxon blood?
Or am I confusing that with the Josefstadt,
Where up and down its narrow Viennese streets
With their German names he walked for weeks on end—
Until the cobblestones tore his shoes apart.
O barefoot pilgrim: it's bound-for-exile Dante
Whose gray-cowled figure appears to you in the crowd.
And you in Verona, stalked by your own paranoia.

And the shade still looking afraid of being burned alive.

*

Picture an open flower: its teeming bud
An ancient city, the splayed petals its sagging,
Meandering walls. A polis-heliotrope
A honeybee now enters, one for whom
Distilled impression is siphoned pollen, still drawn
To what he imagines are the gilded pistils
And purple calyx of ruined Corinth. Until
The next horizon's heliotropic polis
Envelops Pausanias: Athens, Argos, Delphi.

But no highway as high as Pindar's Olympian odes.
And no road to Rhodes, the island that lay in Ocean's
Murky Below—until its name unfolds
Like a flower in Pindar's poem. The mythos told
And retold as logos: *She rose up into the open*
Light in the arms of Helios. But that

Was poetry before there was prose. Before there was Rhodes.

*

"Okay, walk us through it," said the beautiful
Face to the stricken one, on the six o'clock news.
The bodies still exposed . . . Sublime-mundane,
Coterminous slog. Same-old somnambulant, dreadful
Same-old. Like Earth in its orbits, all oxen roads stuck
In ruts of ritual pacing and rote impression.

A daily log that darkens early. Office treadmill.

*

Pomerium. Sacred boundary line around
The city, inscribed by Romulus with the bronze
Blade of a plough. Trenchant furrow for Caesar's
Bloodlines. Virgil's imperial, circumspect poem.
The city lights, at the city limits, ablaze.
And if the walls of seven-walled Troy could speak—
Rudimentary, radical, radial, riddled, redundant
Walls once raised by the gods to be razed by the Greeks—
Would they say to us, as they did to Pausanias,
It's a perilous thing to outlive the end of your myth?
Across so many countries, and over the waves
Of different seas, observing the ancient custom
Of bearing an urn to Ilium's ashen plains,
The closest he could come to what doesn't remain:

Elegiac Catullus, the Troad's older brother.

*

When the Romans and the Aitolians ordered him
To withdraw all of his Macedonian troops
"Beyond the borders of Hellas," Philip V

Offered this apposite rejoinder: *Define Hellas.*

ACKNOWLEDGMENTS

Poems in this book have appeared, some in slightly different versions, in the following publications:

Agni, Arion, Berfrois, Charles River Journal, Consequence, Five Points, Fulcrum, Harvard Review, Ibbetson Street, Levure littériare, Literary Imagination, Literary Matters, Little Star, New Ohio Review, The Oxford Gazette, Poetry Ireland, Pusteblume, The Republic of Letters, Salamander, Slate, Spillway, Vergilius, and *The Warwick Review.*

"Origins" was anthologized in *Joining Music with Reason: 34 Poets, British and American, Oxford 2004–2009* ed. Christopher Ricks, (Oxfordshire: Waywiser Press, 2010).

My version of Pindar's "Olympian 14" first appeared in my book of paired poems in translation, *Dialogos* (Champaign, IL: Antilever, 2012).

Various friends have been exacting and encouraging readers of these poems. I am especially grateful to Jenny Barber, Daniel Bosch, Peter Caputo, Greg Delanty, Richard Fein, Melissa Green, Katherine Jackson, Sarah Kafatou, Marcia Karp, Fred Marchant, Nicholas Racheotes, Dillon Tracy, Rosanna Warren, and Maria Zervos.

NOTES

Guide to Greece: The title of this book comes from the way that Byzantine copyists referred to the work of Pausanias, a second–century (C.E.) Greek prose writer who lived during the time of the *Pax Romana,* when Greece was under Roman control, whose occupation and subjugation had superseded Macedonian dominance. Pausanias' writing served as a guidebook for Roman tourists; its content was chiefly concerned with the sacred sites, and how to get to them, and what one might expect to find there. Much of what he found no longer exists, except in his prose. Over a twenty year period Pausanias traversed nearly the whole of mainland Greece. Some of the sites he visited in Arcadia and Sparta are places of origin familiar to me in connection with my ancestral parentage.

When stress marks appear in the text they are usually placed over Modern Greek words. As unfamiliar as these demotic words are to most readers, and in order to ensure that the meter of the line is maintained, I felt it necessary to include some indicators of pronunciation and versification: signs for hearing the syllables of the words in the rhythm of the lines. In some places, the accent marks and forms of transliteration are meant to reflect the idiomatic Greek as I heard it, growing up.

"Source of the Styx": *the blackened ridge of Psará* is a phrase from the poem by Dionysios Solomos, "The Destruction of Psará" (1825). The inhabitants of this island were massacred during the Greek War of Independence.

"Panopeus": Ancient Panopeus was a famous city. "Over the lovely dancing rings of Panopeus" is from *Odyssey 11,* translated by Robert Fitzgerald.

"The Philippeum (168 B.C.E.)": The Battle of Chaironeia (338 B.C.E.) established the primacy of Macedonia over Greece. The Battle of Pydna (168 B.C.E.) marked the end of Alexander's Macedonian empire and the start of Roman hegemony.

"The Scholars Critique Pausanias' Style": The phrase "*Study the ruins*" is adapted from the refrain in David Ferry's version of *Gilgamesh:* "Study the brickwork, study the fortification." (New York: Farrar, Straus, and Giroux, 1993).

"Austerity Measures I": *Pappoúli* is vernacular Greek for grandfather.

"Argonauts": My rendition of Seferis' poem omits the opening quote from Plato (*Alcibiades 133b*) and the final word of the last line, *Dikaiosune* (Justice).

"Mycenae: Pausanias Conducts a Guided Tour of the Burial Chambers": *"As heavy as the ox on the watchman's tongue"* is an allusion to Aeschylus' *Agamemnon*.

"Franklin Park Zoo": *Moréklavé* means something like "milksop."

"Peregrinations of Pausanias": "To live past the end of your myth is a perilous thing." Anne Carson's *Red Doc* (New York: Knopf, 2013).

"Tibullus in Sparta": In accord with the pastoral context of this poem, I have used the ancient word for sheep, *probata*, rather than the modern *provata*.

CPSIA information can be obtained
at www.ICGtesting.com
Printed in the USA
LVHW011750271118
598427LV00005B/525

9 780807 168417